WAYLAND
ATLAS OF THE WORLD

Wayland

Canadian edition
First published in 1983 by
Nelson Canada
A Division of International Thomson Limited
1120 Birchmount Road, Scarborough
Ontario M1K 5G4, Canada

© Copyright Nelson Canada
A Division of International Thomson Limited, 1983

UK edition
First published in 1985 by
Wayland (Publishers) Limited
61 Western Road, Hove
East Sussex BN3 1JD, England

Reprinted (with revision) 1988
Completely revised edition 1994

Maps on pages 6–7 and 32–43
© Copyright 1985 Wayland (Publishers) Ltd

Hardback ISBN 0 7502 1121 0

Paperback ISBN 0 7502 1122 9

Printed and bound in Italy by
G. Canale & C.S.p.A., Turin

Educational Consultant:
Ben Vass, Co-ordinator of Geography
North York Board of Education, Ontario, Canada

Educational Consultant on UK edition:
Dr L. Bolwell, Brighton Polytechnic
Falmer, Sussex

Charts and graphs by Mary Jane Gerber
Revised and updated by Malcolm S. Walker
Completely revised edition:
Merle and Alan Thompson

The author wishes to thank cartographers Hedy Later,
Jane Davie and Julia Sandquist for their splendid work,
and Helena Matthews for her remarkable patience.

CONTENTS

INTRODUCTION

Using Your Atlas

This atlas has been prepared to help you understand more about the world and each of its regions. The large, clear maps will help you find out more about the world we live in.

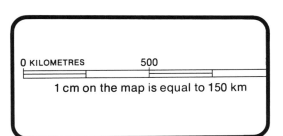

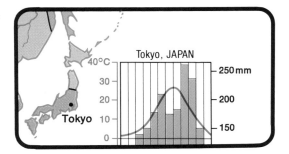

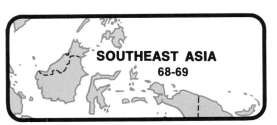

hurricane: the name given to violent sto the late summer and autumn in the Wes Caribbean.

Country	Population	
United Kingdom	57 237 000	
India	827 057 000	
Bangladesh	115 593 000	

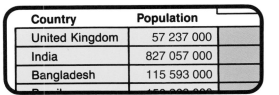

Abadan, Iran **66** 3E
Aberdeen, U.K. **54** 3E
Abidjan, Ivory Coast **58** 7D
Abilene, U.S.A. **48** 5F
Abu Dhabi, United Arab Emirates **66** 5F

Direction

It is normal for maps to be drawn with North at the top of the page, and this is so in this atlas. To help you, some maps have an arrow that points towards the North.

Scale

Every map is drawn to a scale. A scale lets you measure the distance from one place to another and gives you some idea of size. It tells what distance on earth is represented by a certain distance on the map. On the world maps, the scale is shown as a written statement only. On the British and European maps and the regional maps, the scale is shown as a written statement and as a divided bar to help you measure distances.

World Pattern Maps

The first set of sixteen maps gives you specialized information about the earth. They use a variety of symbols and colours and have been chosen to let you study such topics as physical landforms, transportation, climate, population, energy, and land use. They can be read and understood only by studying the legend on each map. Here it is explained what the symbols stand for. You can look at the Table of Contents on page iii to find the map dealing with the topic you want.

British and European Maps

This set of ten maps gives you a closer view of Britain and Europe than you could get in the world pattern map section. In this section, the topics are landforms, climate, farming, administration, population, minerals, North Sea oil and gas, and economic co-operation.

Regional Maps

This set of fifteen maps gives you a more detailed picture of each region of the world. Each map lets you study the political divisions, rivers, and transportation links in the region, and shows you as many cities as possible without making the maps too crowded. Check the index map on pages 44–45 to find the particular region you want to study.

Glossary

Some of the words or terms that are used on the maps may be new and unfamiliar to you. You can learn the meaning of these by looking them up in the Glossary on pages 74–75.

Statistics, Charts, and Graphs

The maps in this atlas give you a great deal of useful information about the world. On pages 76–83 we show you other ways in which geographical information can be recorded and displayed. We think you will find these facts and figures both interesting and helpful for all kinds of social studies projects.

Index

The alphabetical index on pages 84–92 helps you find places and physical features shown in the atlas. It also tells you where a place is located on each map.

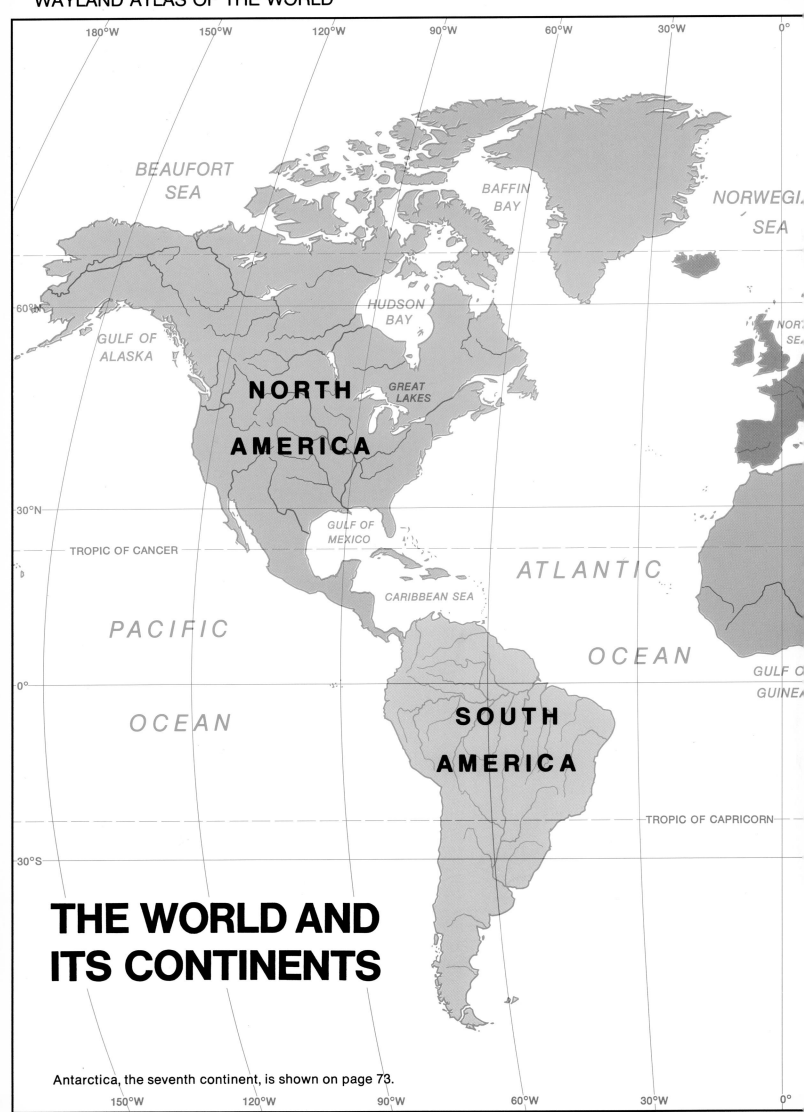

180°W 150°W 120°W 90°W 60°W 30°W 0°

BEAUFORT SEA

BAFFIN BAY

NORWEGIAN SEA

60°N

HUDSON BAY

NORTH SEA

GULF OF ALASKA

NORTH AMERICA

GREAT LAKES

30°N

GULF OF MEXICO

TROPIC OF CANCER

ATLANTIC

CARIBBEAN SEA

OCEAN

GULF OF GUINEA

PACIFIC

0°

OCEAN

SOUTH AMERICA

TROPIC OF CAPRICORN

30°S

THE WORLD AND ITS CONTINENTS

Antarctica, the seventh continent, is shown on page 73.

150°W 120°W 90°W 60°W 30°W 0°

ARCTIC OCEAN

LAPTEV SEA

ARCTIC CIRCLE

60°N

EUROPE

BALTIC SEA

SEA OF OKHOTSK

BLACK SEA

ASIA

SEA OF JAPAN

CASPIAN SEA

MEDITERRANEAN SEA

30°N

PERSIAN GULF

PACIFIC

RED SEA

AFRICA

ARABIAN SEA

BAY OF BENGAL

SOUTH CHINA SEA

OCEAN

INDIAN

TIMOR SEA

CORAL SEA

EQUATOR

0°

OCEAN

AUSTRALASIA

30°S

TASMAN SEA

30°E   60°E   90°E   120°E   150°E   180°E

1 cm on the map is equal to 800 km at the equator

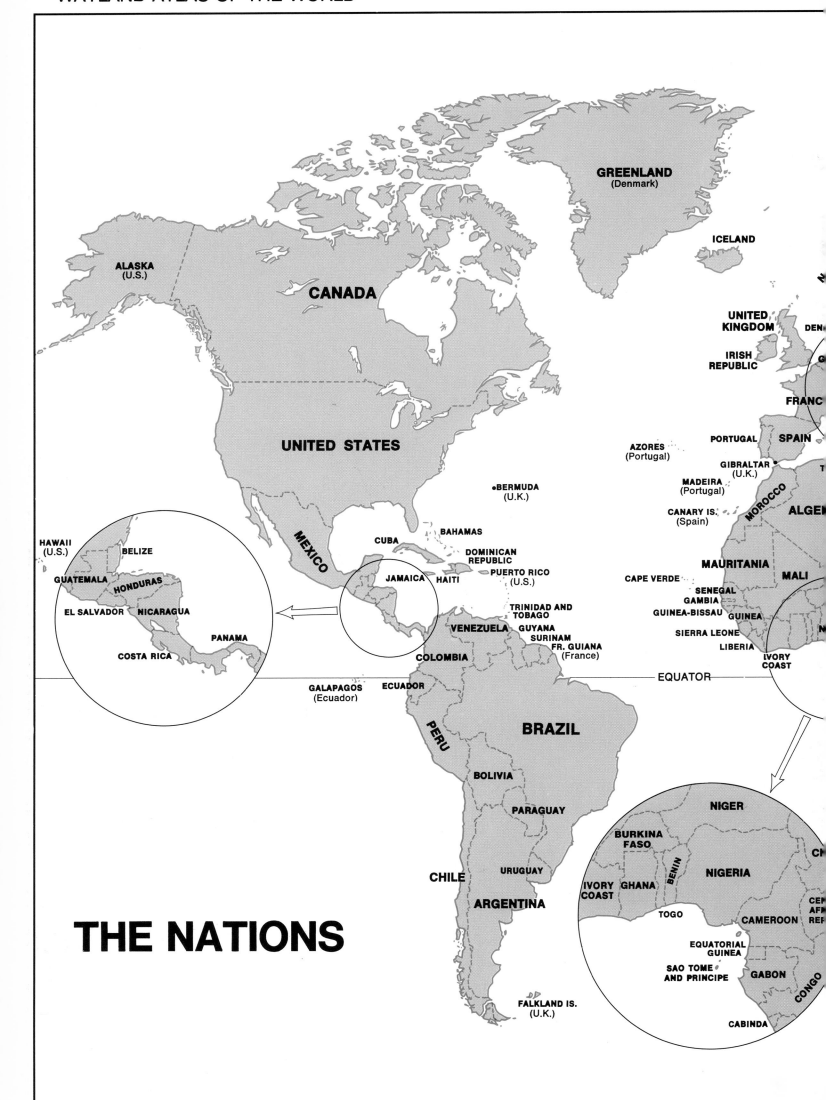

GREENLAND
(Denmark)

ICELAND

ALASKA
(U.S.)

CANADA

UNITED
KINGDOM   DEN

IRISH
REPUBLIC

FRANC

AZORES
(Portugal)   PORTUGAL   SPAIN

GIBRALTAR
(U.K.)

MADEIRA
(Portugal)

●BERMUDA
(U.K.)

UNITED STATES

CANARY IS.
(Spain)

MOROCCO   ALGE

BAHAMAS

HAWAII
(U.S.)

BELIZE

GUATEMALA

HONDURAS

EL SALVADOR   NICARAGUA

COSTA RICA

PANAMA

CUBA

DOMINICAN
REPUBLIC

PUERTO RICO
(U.S.)

JAMAICA   HAITI

MEXICO

MAURITANIA   MALI

CAPE VERDE

SENEGAL
GAMBIA
GUINEA-BISSAU   GUINEA

SIERRA LEONE

LIBERIA

IVORY
COAST

TRINIDAD AND
TOBAGO

VENEZUELA   GUYANA
SURINAM
FR. GUIANA
(France)

COLOMBIA

GALAPAGOS
(Ecuador)

ECUADOR

EQUATOR

PERU

BRAZIL

BOLIVIA

PARAGUAY

NIGER

BURKINA
FASO

IVORY   GHANA
COAST

BENIN

NIGERIA

CH

CE
AF
RE

CHILE

URUGUAY

ARGENTINA

TOGO

CAMEROON

EQUATORIAL
GUINEA

SAO TOME
AND PRINCIPE

GABON

CONGO

THE NATIONS

FALKLAND IS.
(U.K.)

CABINDA

RUSSIA

NETHERLANDS
BYELORUSS
BELGIUM
GERMANY
POLAND
LUXEMBOURG
CZECH REP.
UKRAINE
SLOVAKIA
AUSTRIA
HUNGARY
MOLDAVA
SWITZERLAND
FRANCE
ROMANIA
1
2
ITALY
3
5
CORSICA (France)
4
BULGARIA
SARDINIA (Italy)
ALBANIA
6
ALBANIA
GREECE
SICILY (Italy)

1 SLOVENIA
2 CROATIA
3 BOSNIA-HERZEGOVINA
4 MONTENEGRO
5 SERBIA
6 MACEDONIA

SVALBARD (Norway)

FINLAND

ESTONIA
LATVIA
LITHUANIA
LAND

UKRAINE

R U S S I A

K A Z A K H S T A N

MONGOLIA

GEORGIA
ARMENIA
UZBEKISTAN
TURKMENISTAN
KIRGIZIA
TURKEY
AZER-BAIJAN
TADZHIKISTAN
NORTH KOREA
JAPAN

ALTA
CYPRUS
SYRIA
LEBANON
ISRAEL
IRAQ
IRAN
AFGHAN-ISTAN
CHINA
SOUTH KOREA

BYA
EGYPT
JORDAN
SAUDI ARABIA
PAKISTAN
NEPAL
BHUTAN
TAIWAN

CHAD
SUDAN
INDIA
BANGLADESH
MYANMAR
HONG KONG (U.K.)

C.A.R.
ETHIOPIA
SOMALIA
LAOS
THAILAND
VIETNAM
PHILIPPINES
ANDAMAN IS. (India)
CAMBODIA

UGANDA
KENYA
SRI LANKA
BRUNEI

RWANDA
ZAIRE
BURUNDI
MALDIVES
MALAYSIA
SINGAPORE

TANZANIA
SEYCHELLES
INDONESIA
PAPUA-NEW GUINEA
SOLOMON IS.

GOLA
MALAWI
ZAMBIA
MADAGASCAR
MAURITIUS
VANUATU

ZIMBABWE
REUNION
NEW CALEDONIA (France)
BOTSWANA
SWAZILAND
AUSTRALIA
SOUTH AFRICA
LESOTHO

IRAQ
IRAN
KUWAIT
BAHRAIN
QATAR
SAUDI ARABIA
UNITED ARAB EMIRATES
OMAN
ERITREA
YEMEN REP.
ETHIOPIA
DJIBOUTI
SOMALIA

NEW ZEALAND

1 cm on the map is equal to 800 km at the equator

GREENLAND
(Denmark)

ICELAND

ALASKA
(U.S.)

CANADA

UNITED
KINGDOM

IRISH
REPUBLIC

FRANCE

PORTUGAL SPAIN

UNITED STATES

AZORES
(Portugal)

GIBRALTAR
(U.K.)

TUN

MADEIRA
(Portugal)

MOROCCO

ALGERI

•BERMUDA
(U.K.)

CANARY IS.
(Spain)

HAWAII
(U.S.)

MEXICO

BAHAMAS

CUBA

1 BELIZE
2 GUATEMALA
3 HONDURAS
4 EL SALVADOR
5 NICARAGUA
6 COSTA RICA
7 PANAMA

DOMINICAN
REPUBLIC

PUERTO RICO

JAMAICA HAITI

MAURITANIA

CAPE VERDE

SENEGAL
GAMBIA
GUINEA-BISSAU GUINEA

MALI

1

TRINIDAD AND
TOBAGO

SIERRA LEONE IVORY
COAST

2

3
4

N

VENEZUELA GUYANA
SURINAM

LIBERIA

COLOMBIA

FR. GUIANA
(France)

GALAPAGOS IS.
(Ecuador)

ECUADOR

EQUATOR

1 BURKINA FASO
2 GHANA
3 TOGO
4 BENIN
5 CAMEROON
6 CENTRAL AFRICAN RE
7 EQUATORIAL GUINEA
8 GABON
9 CONGO
10 SAO TOME & PRINCIPE
11 CABINDA

1

MAJOR INTERNATIONAL ORGANIZATIONS

PERU

BRAZIL

BOLIVIA

PARAGUAY

CHILE

URUGUAY

ARGENTINA

The Commonwealth

European Community (EC)

Commonwealth of Independent States

Organization of American States

Arab League

Communist States

FALKLAND IS.
(U.K.)

Association of South East Asian States

Nations not members of these organizations

For explanation of these terms see glossary

SVALBARD
(Norway)

FINLAND

RUSSIA

UKRAINE

KAZAKHSTAN

MONGOLIA

GEORGIA
ARMENIA AZER
BAIJAN
TURKEY
UZBEKISTAN
KIRGIZIA
TURKMENISTAN
TADZHIKISTAN

NORTH
KOREA

JAPAN

CYPRUS
LEBANON
ISRAEL
SYRIA
IRAQ
IRAN
AFGHAN-
ISTAN
PAKISTAN
JORDAN

CHINA

SOUTH
KOREA

MALTA

LIBYA

EGYPT

SAUDI
ARABIA

OMAN

NEPAL
BHUTAN

BANGLADESH

INDIA

MYANMAR

LAOS

TAIWAN

HONG KONG
(U.K.)

VIETNAM

PHILIPPINES

CHAD

SUDAN

YEMEN

6

5

ANDAMAN
IS. (India)

THAILAND

CAMBODIA

1 KUWAIT
2 BAHRAIN
3 QATAR
4 UNITED ARAB EMIRATES
5 DJIBOUTI
6 ERITREA

C.A.R.

ETHIOPIA

SOMALIA

SRI
LANKA

BRUNEI
MALAYSIA

UGANDA
KENYA

MALDIVES

RWANDA
ZAIRE
BURUNDI

SINGAPORE

SEYCHELLES

TANZANIA

INDONESIA

PAPUA-
NEW GUINEA

SOLOMON IS.

ANGOLA

MALAWI

ZAMBIA

MOZAMBIQUE

MADAGASCAR

MAURITIUS

VANUATU

NAMBIA
ZIMBABWE

BOTSWANA

REUNION

NEW
CALEDONIA
(France)

AUSTRALIA

SWAZILAND

SOUTH
AFRICA
LESOTHO

NEW
ZEALAND

Inset map (Europe)

NORWAY

SWEDEN

ESTONIA

UNITED
KINGDOM

DENMARK

LATVIA

LITHUANIA

1

BYELORUSS

THE
NETHERLANDS
GERMANY
BELGIUM

POLAND

LUXEMBOURG

CZECH
REP.
SLOVAKIA

UKRAINE

FRANCE
SWITZ.
AUSTRIA
HUNGARY

MOLDAVA

2
3

ROMANIA

ITALY

4

SERBIA

5

BULGARIA

6

ALBANIA

GREECE

TURKEY

1 RUSSIA
2 SLOVENIA
3 CROATIA
4 BOSNIA-HERZEGOVINA
5 MONTENEGRO
6 MACEDONIA

1 cm on the map is equal to 800 km at the equator

5

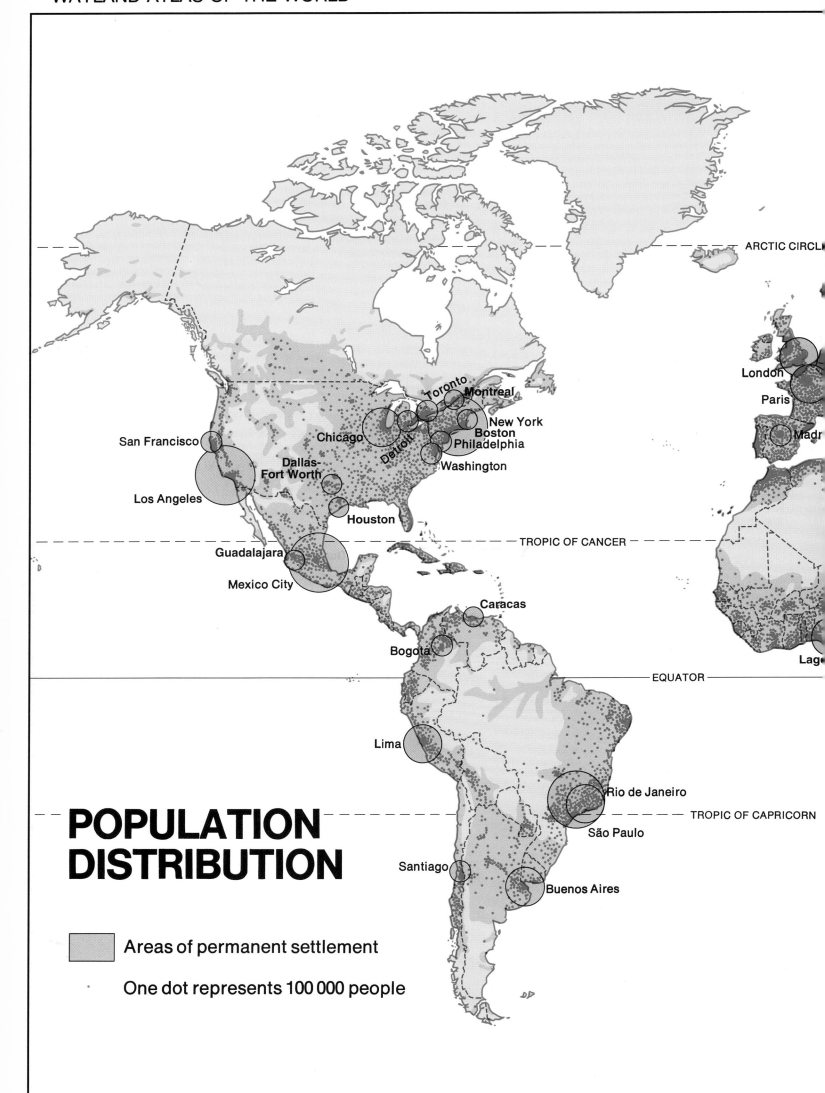

ARCTIC CIRCL

London

Paris

Madr

TROPIC OF CANCER

Lag

EQUATOR

Toronto
Montreal
New York
Boston
Chicago
Philadelphia
Detroit
Washington
San Francisco
Dallas-
Fort Worth
Los Angeles
Houston
Guadalajara
Mexico City
Caracas
Bogota
Lima
Rio de Janeiro
São Paulo
Santiago
Buenos Aires

TROPIC OF CAPRICORN

POPULATION DISTRIBUTION

Areas of permanent settlement

One dot represents 100 000 people

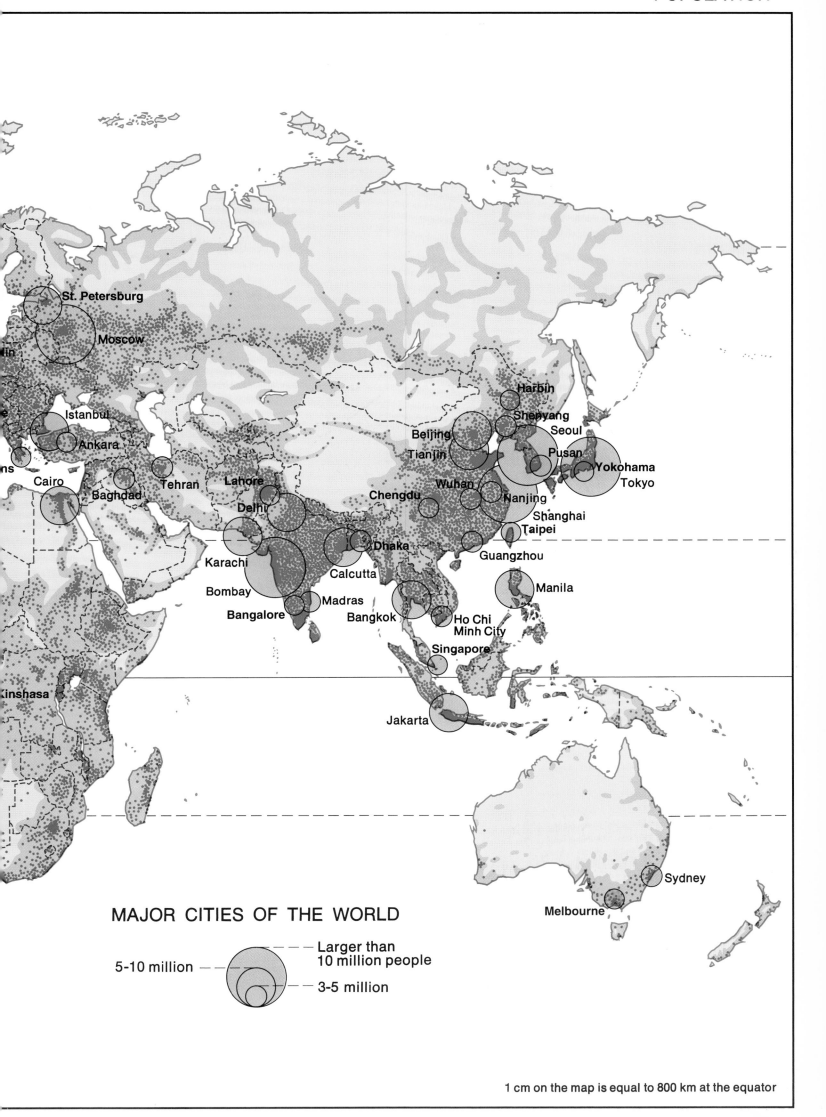

St. Petersburg

Moscow

Istanbul

Ankara

Cairo

Baghdad

Tehran

Lahore

Delhi

Karachi

Bombay

Bangalore

Madras

Calcutta

Dhaka

Bangkok

Ho Chi
Minh City

Singapore

Jakarta

Kinshasa

Harbin

Shenyang

Beijing

Tianjin

Seoul

Pusan

Yokohama

Tokyo

Wuhan

Chengdu

Nanjing

Shanghai

Taipei

Guangzhou

Manila

Sydney

Melbourne

MAJOR CITIES OF THE WORLD

5-10 million

Larger than
10 million people

3-5 million

1 cm on the map is equal to 800 km at the equator

7

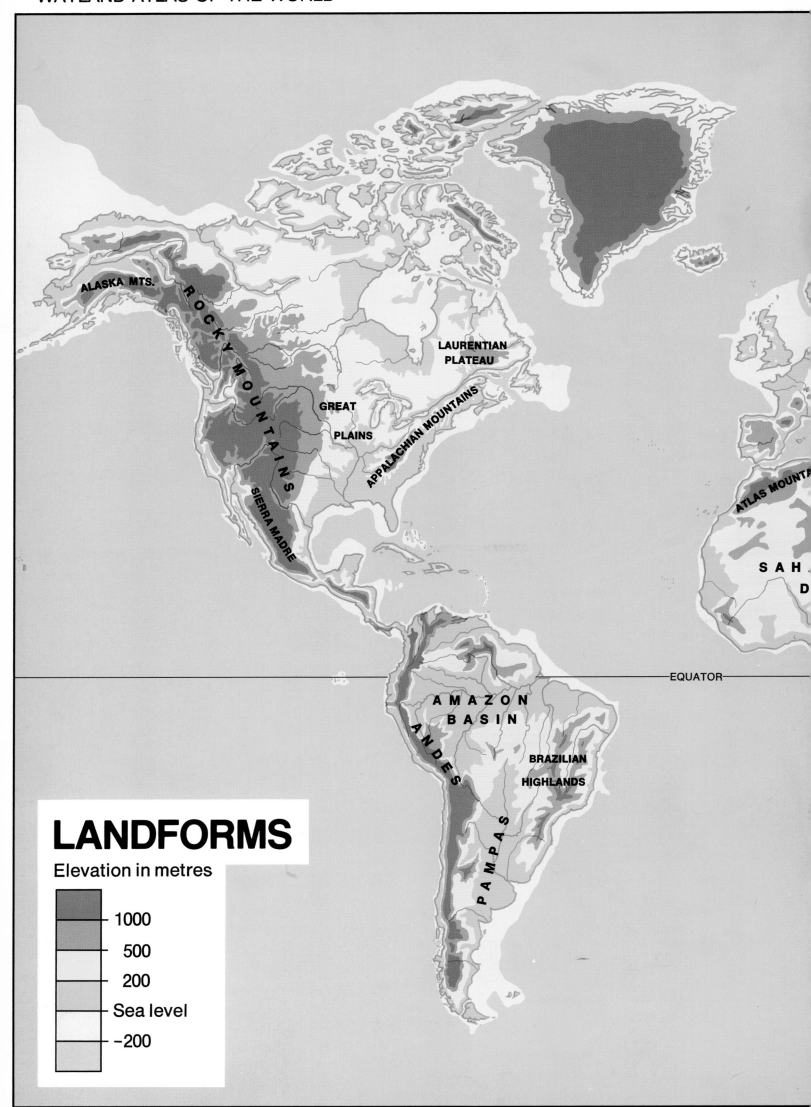

ALASKA MTS.

ROCKY MOUNTAINS

LAURENTIAN
PLATEAU

GREAT

PLAINS

APPALACHIAN MOUNTAINS

SIERRA MADRE

ATLAS MOUNTA

S A H

D

EQUATOR

A M A Z O N
B A S I N

ANDES

BRAZILIAN

HIGHLANDS

PAMPAS

LANDFORMS

Elevation in metres

1000

500

200

Sea level

−200

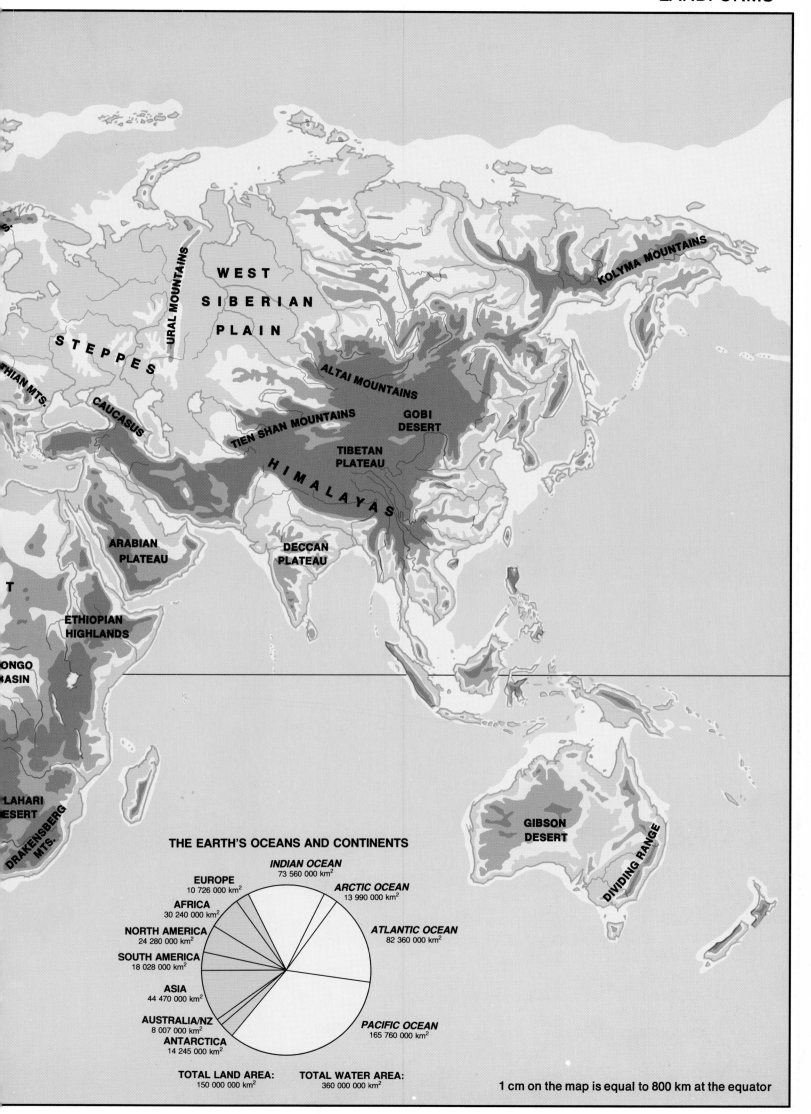

WEST SIBERIAN PLAIN

URAL MOUNTAINS

STEPPES

CAUCASUS

THIAN MTS.

KOLYMA MOUNTAINS

ALTAI MOUNTAINS

TIEN SHAN MOUNTAINS

GOBI DESERT

TIBETAN PLATEAU

HIMALAYAS

ARABIAN PLATEAU

DECCAN PLATEAU

ETHIOPIAN HIGHLANDS

ONGO ASIN

T

LAHARI ESERT

DRAKENSBERG MTS.

GIBSON DESERT

DIVIDING RANGE

THE EARTH'S OCEANS AND CONTINENTS

INDIAN OCEAN
73 560 000 km²

EUROPE
10 726 000 km²

ARCTIC OCEAN
13 990 000 km²

AFRICA
30 240 000 km²

NORTH AMERICA
24 280 000 km²

ATLANTIC OCEAN
82 360 000 km²

SOUTH AMERICA
18 028 000 km²

ASIA
44 470 000 km²

AUSTRALIA/NZ
8 007 000 km²

ANTARCTICA
14 245 000 km²

PACIFIC OCEAN
165 760 000 km²

TOTAL LAND AREA:
150 000 000 km²

TOTAL WATER AREA:
360 000 000 km²

1 cm on the map is equal to 800 km at the equator

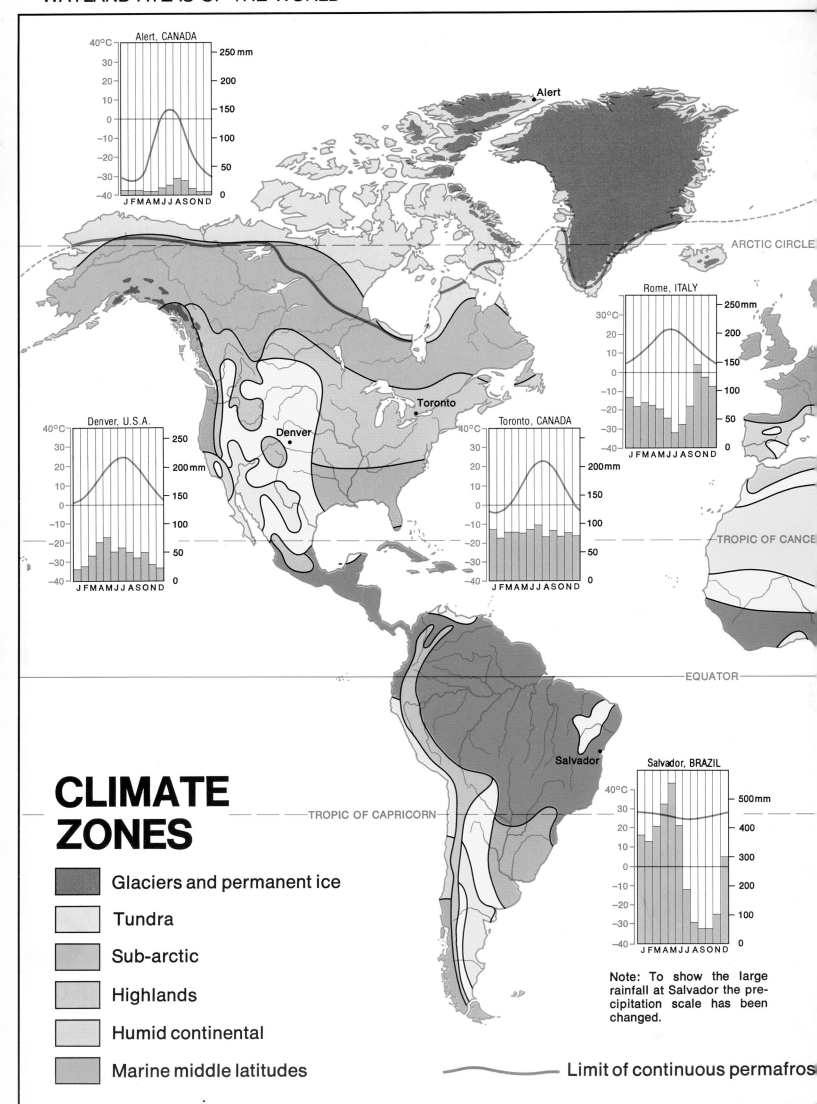

Alert, CANADA

Denver, U.S.A.

Toronto, CANADA

Rome, ITALY

Salvador, BRAZIL

ARCTIC CIRCLE

TROPIC OF CANCER

EQUATOR

TROPIC OF CAPRICORN

CLIMATE ZONES

Glaciers and permanent ice

Tundra

Sub-arctic

Highlands

Humid continental

Marine middle latitudes

Note: To show the large rainfall at Salvador the precipitation scale has been changed.

Limit of continuous permafrost

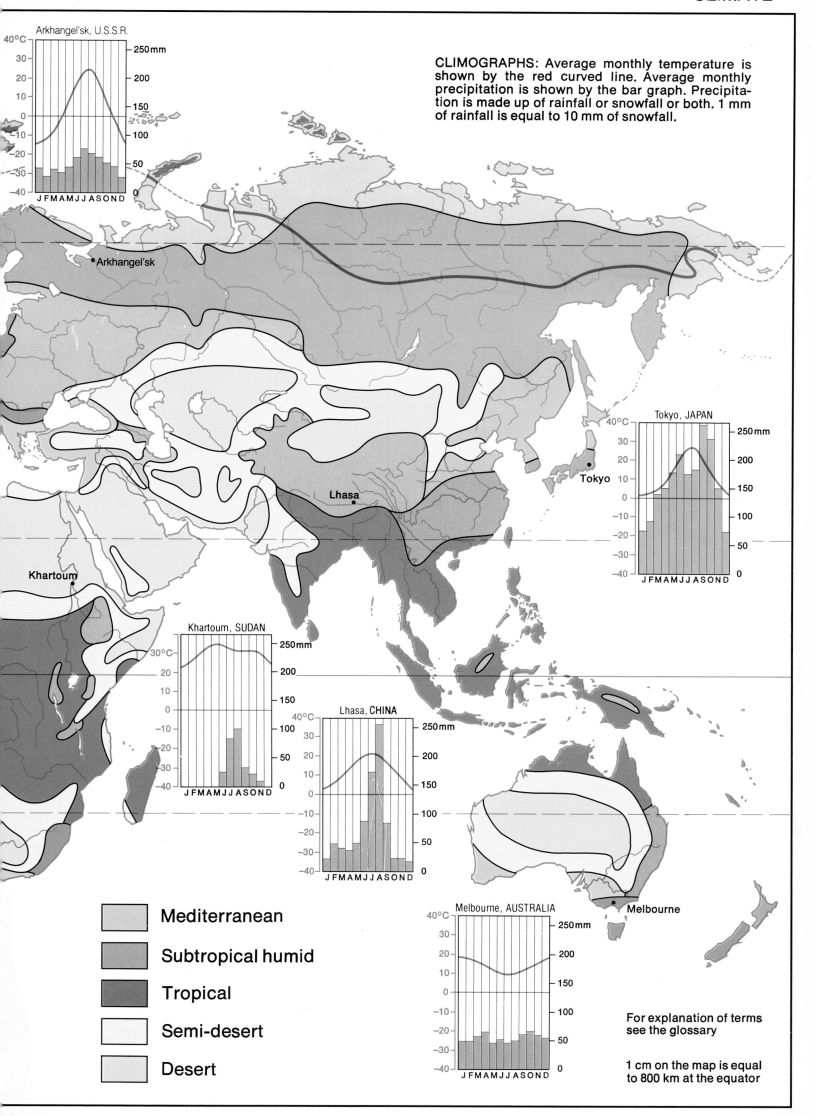

Arkhangel'sk, U.S.S.R.

CLIMOGRAPHS: Average monthly temperature is shown by the red curved line. Average monthly precipitation is shown by the bar graph. Precipitation is made up of rainfall or snowfall or both. 1 mm of rainfall is equal to 10 mm of snowfall.

Tokyo, JAPAN

Khartoum, SUDAN

Lhasa, CHINA

Melbourne, AUSTRALIA

Mediterranean

Subtropical humid

Tropical

Semi-desert

Desert

For explanation of terms see the glossary

1 cm on the map is equal to 800 km at the equator

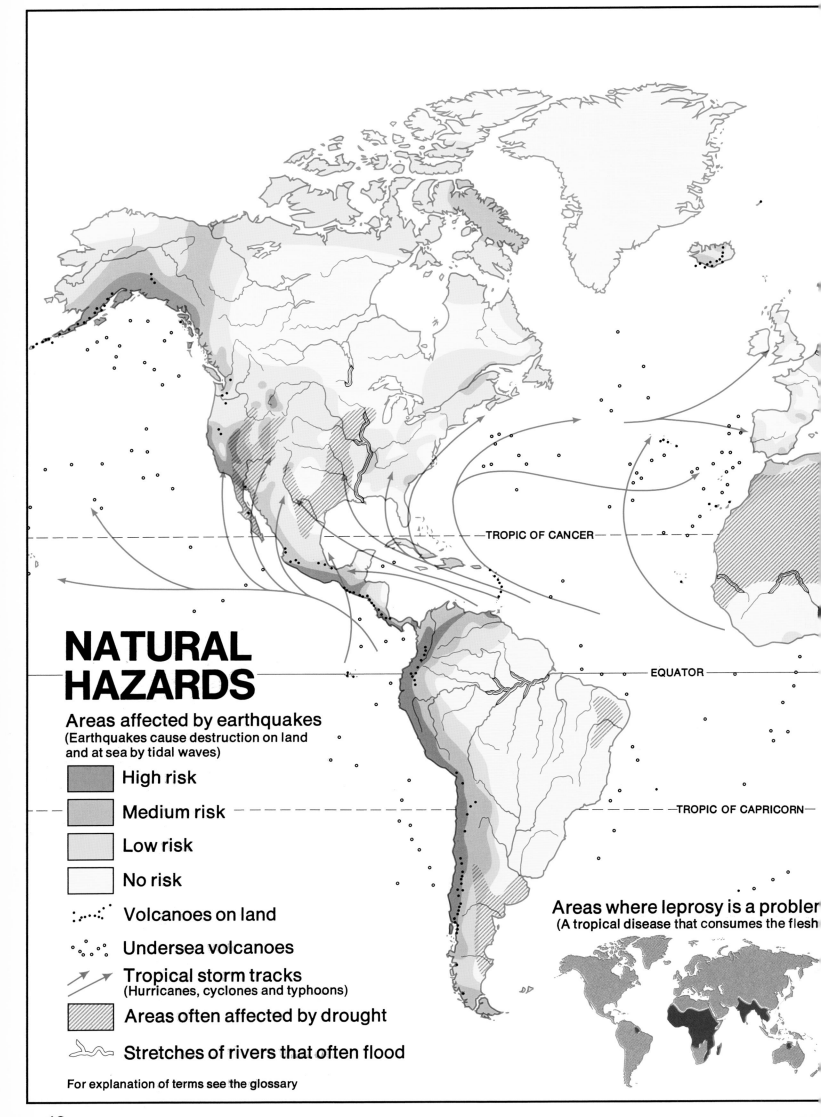

NATURAL HAZARDS

Areas affected by earthquakes
(Earthquakes cause destruction on land and at sea by tidal waves)

High risk

Medium risk

Low risk

No risk

:·...:· Volcanoes on land

°·.°.° Undersea volcanoes

Tropical storm tracks
(Hurricanes, cyclones and typhoons)

Areas often affected by drought

Stretches of rivers that often flood

For explanation of terms see the glossary

TROPIC OF CANCER

EQUATOR

TROPIC OF CAPRICORN

Areas where leprosy is a problem
(A tropical disease that consumes the flesh)

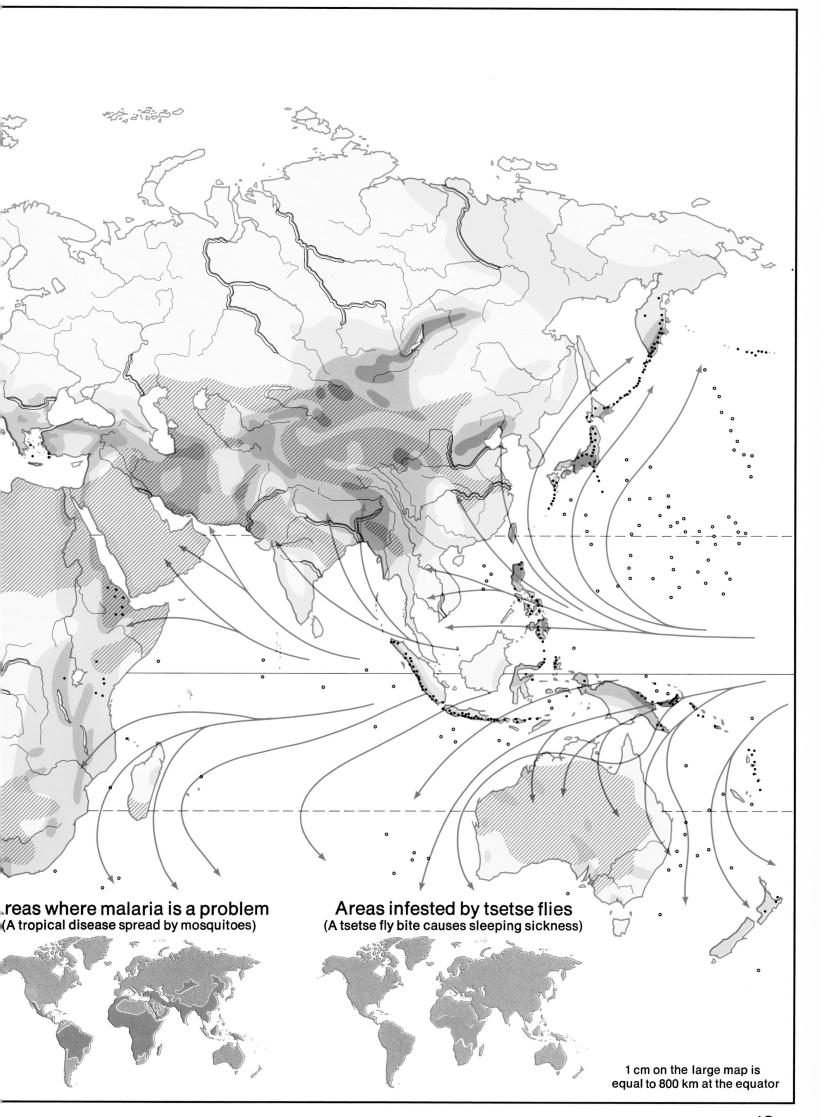

reas where malaria is a problem
(A tropical disease spread by mosquitoes)

Areas infested by tsetse flies
(A tsetse fly bite causes sleeping sickness)

1 cm on the large map is
equal to 800 km at the equator

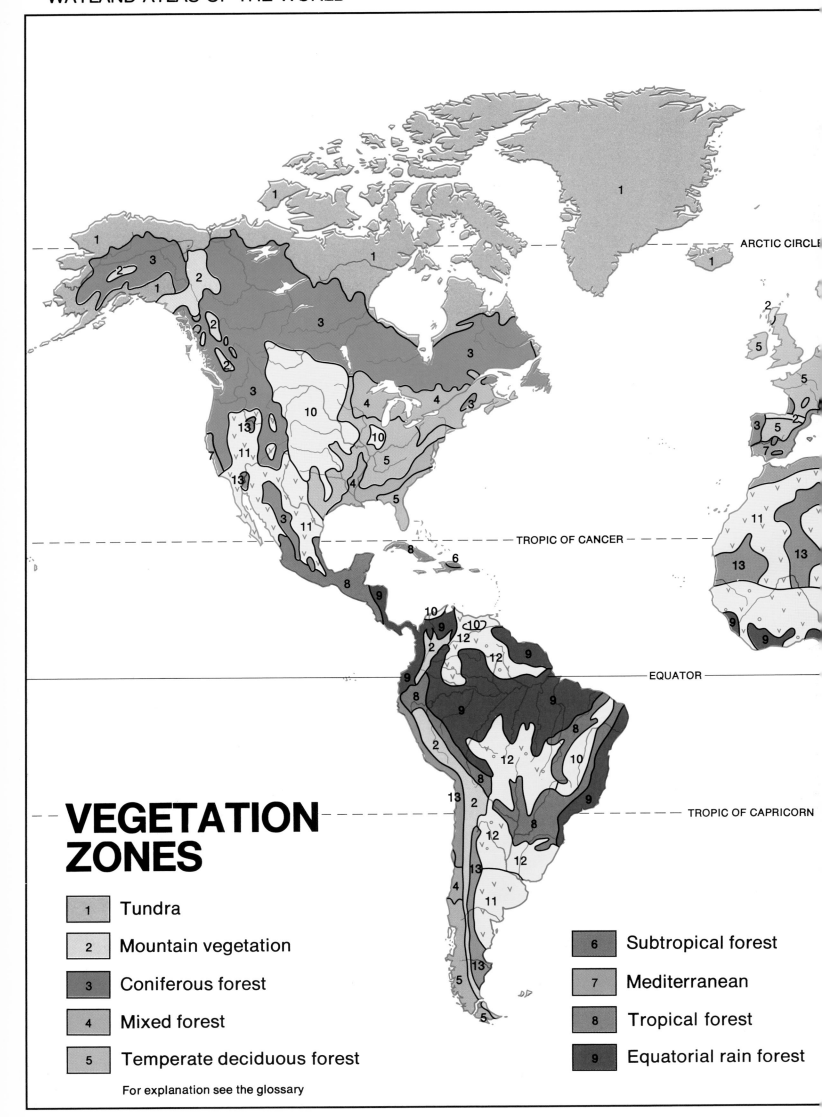

ARCTIC CIRCLE

TROPIC OF CANCER

EQUATOR

TROPIC OF CAPRICORN

VEGETATION
ZONES

1	Tundra
2	Mountain vegetation
3	Coniferous forest
4	Mixed forest
5	Temperate deciduous forest

For explanation see the glossary

6	Subtropical forest
7	Mediterranean
8	Tropical forest
9	Equatorial rain forest

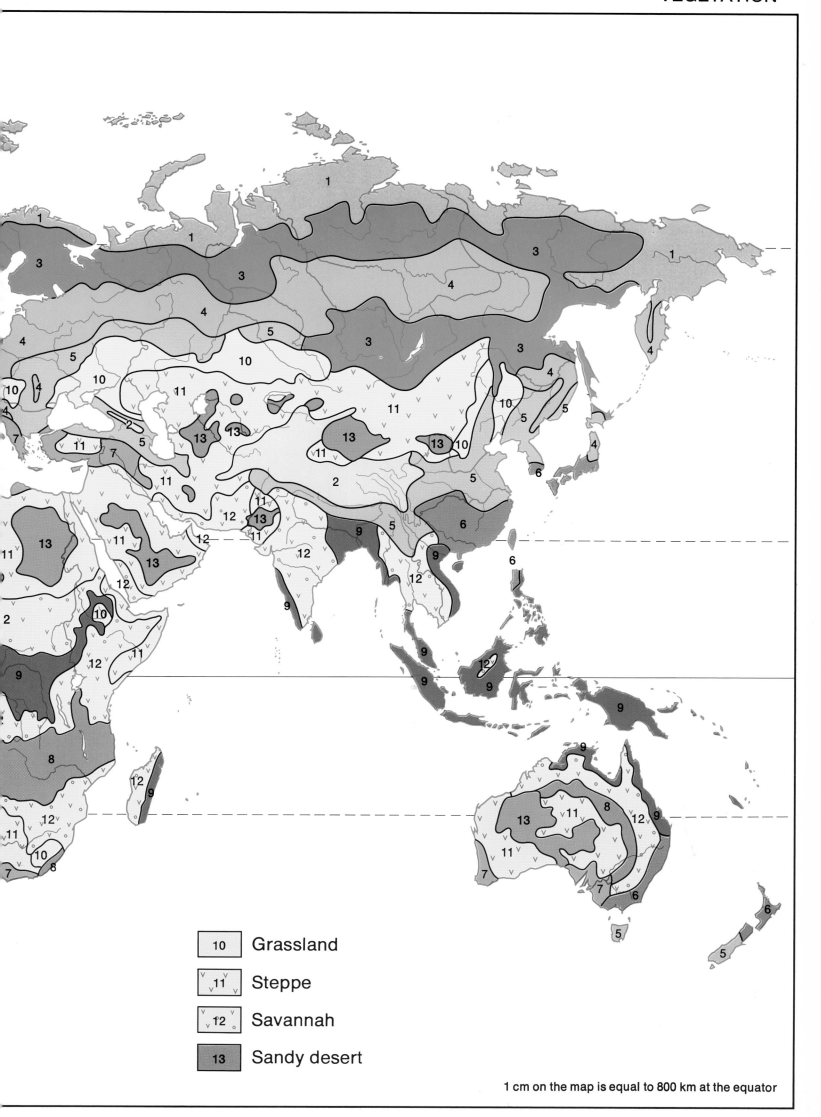

10 Grassland

v 11 v Steppe

v 12 o Savannah

13 Sandy desert

1 cm on the map is equal to 800 km at the equator

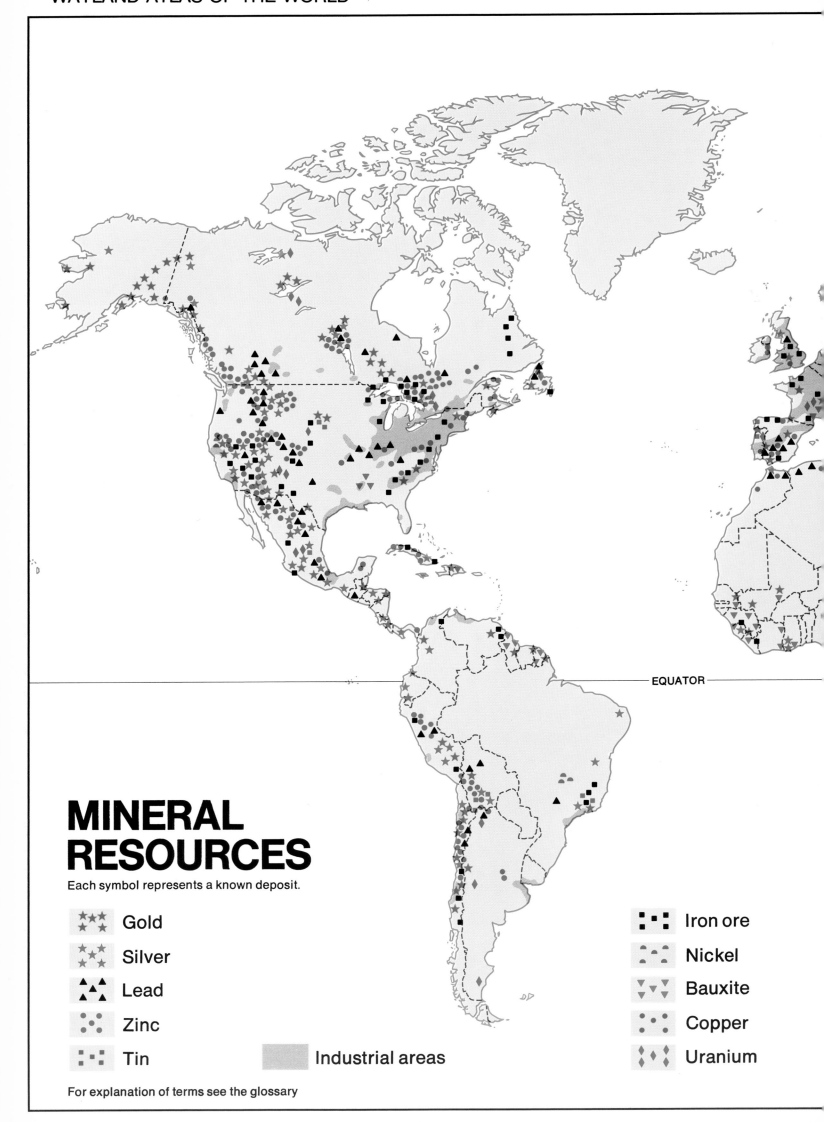

MINERAL RESOURCES

Each symbol represents a known deposit.

★ Gold

★ Silver

▲ Lead

● Zinc

■ Tin

Industrial areas

EQUATOR

■ Iron ore

▲ Nickel

▼ Bauxite

● Copper

◆ Uranium

For explanation of terms see the glossary

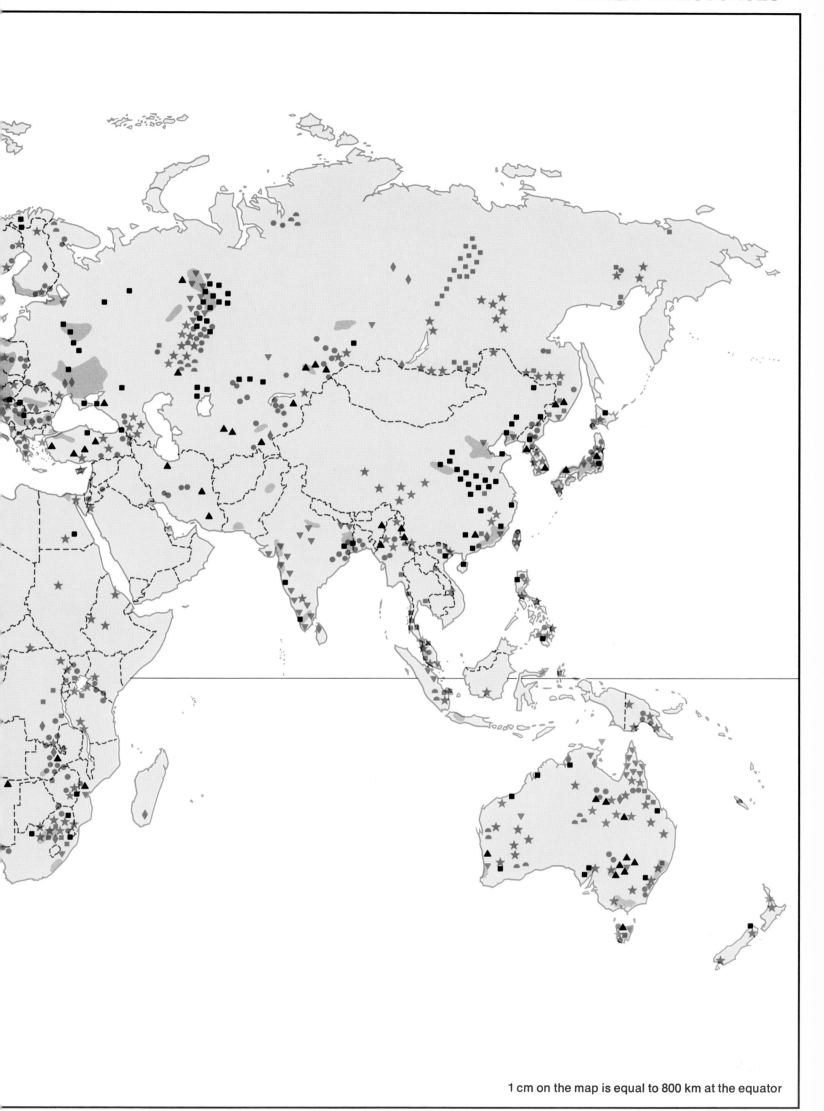

1 cm on the map is equal to 800 km at the equator

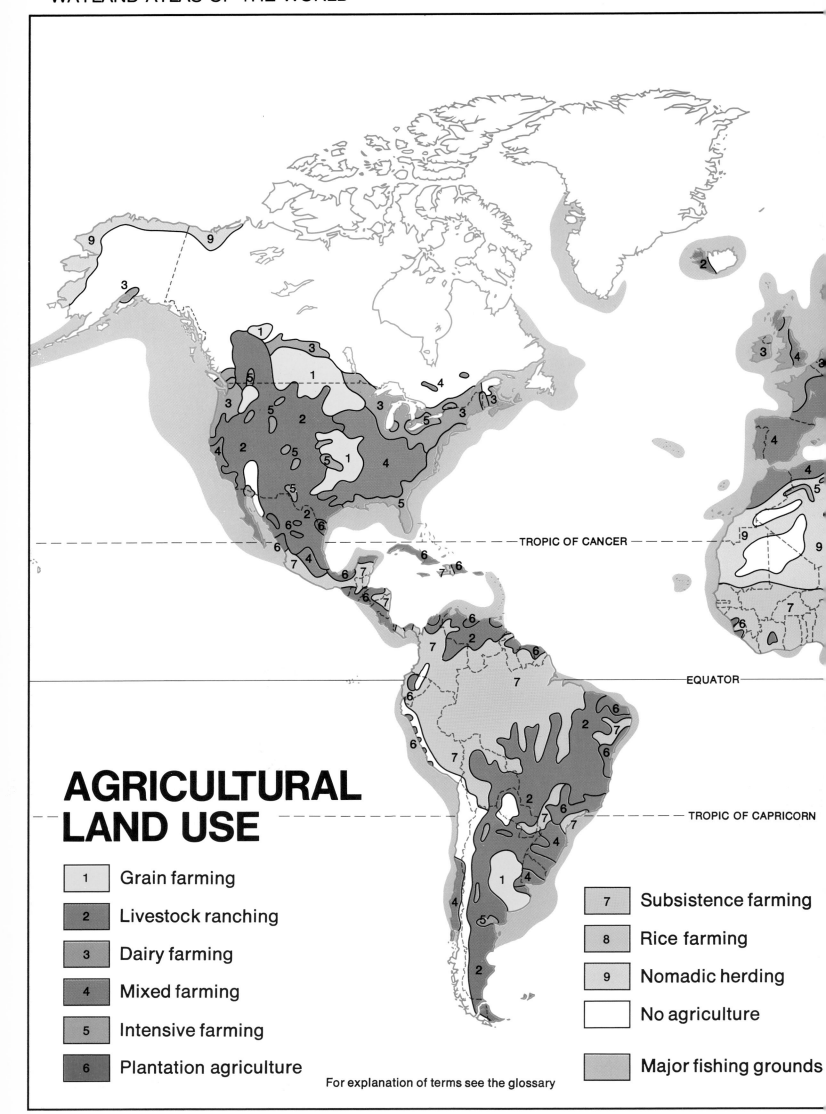

AGRICULTURAL LAND USE

1	Grain farming
2	Livestock ranching
3	Dairy farming
4	Mixed farming
5	Intensive farming
6	Plantation agriculture

7	Subsistence farming
8	Rice farming
9	Nomadic herding
	No agriculture
	Major fishing grounds

For explanation of terms see the glossary

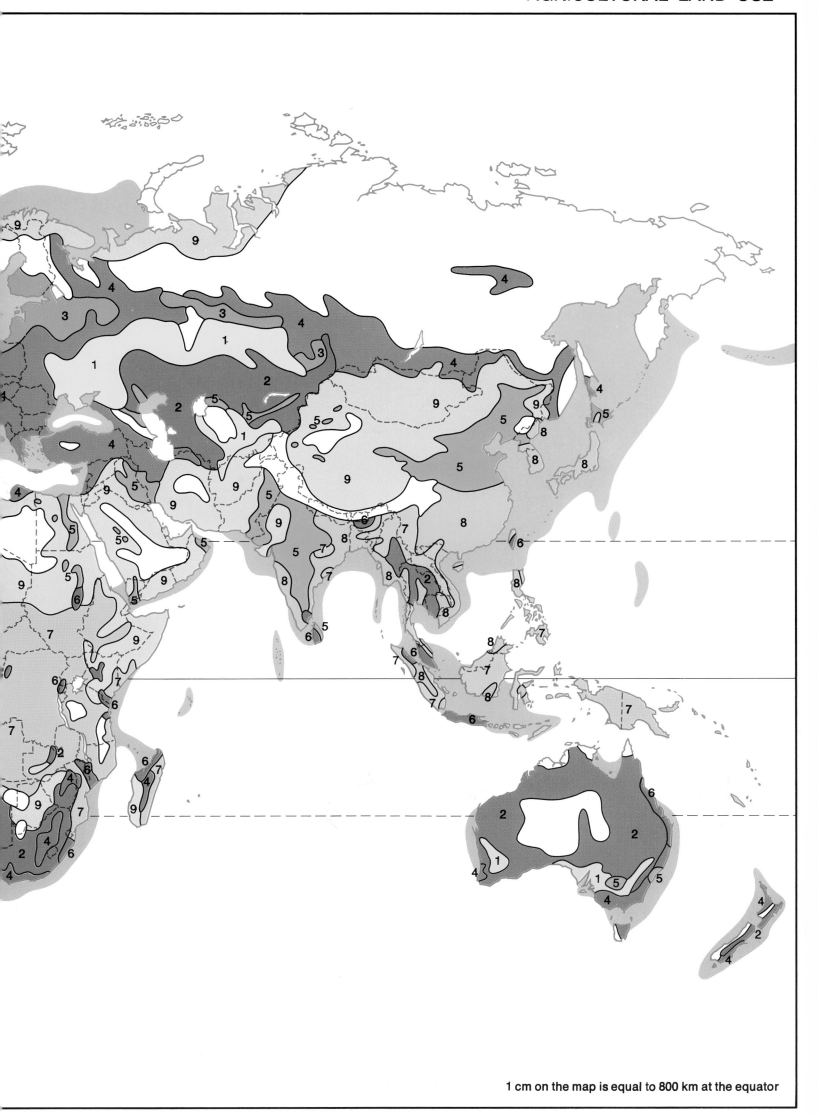

1 cm on the map is equal to 800 km at the equator

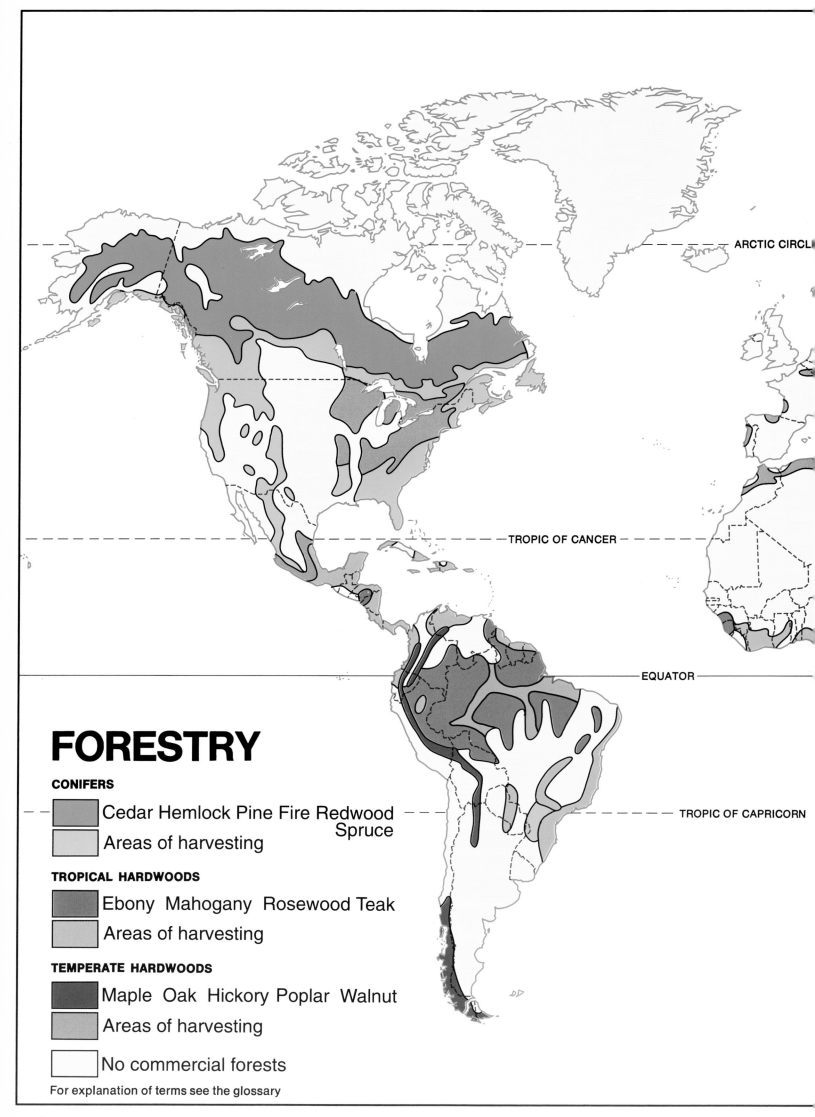

ARCTIC CIRCL

TROPIC OF CANCER

EQUATOR

FORESTRY

CONIFERS

Cedar Hemlock Pine Fire Redwood Spruce

Areas of harvesting

TROPICAL HARDWOODS

Ebony Mahogany Rosewood Teak

Areas of harvesting

TEMPERATE HARDWOODS

Maple Oak Hickory Poplar Walnut

Areas of harvesting

No commercial forests

For explanation of terms see the glossary

TROPIC OF CAPRICORN

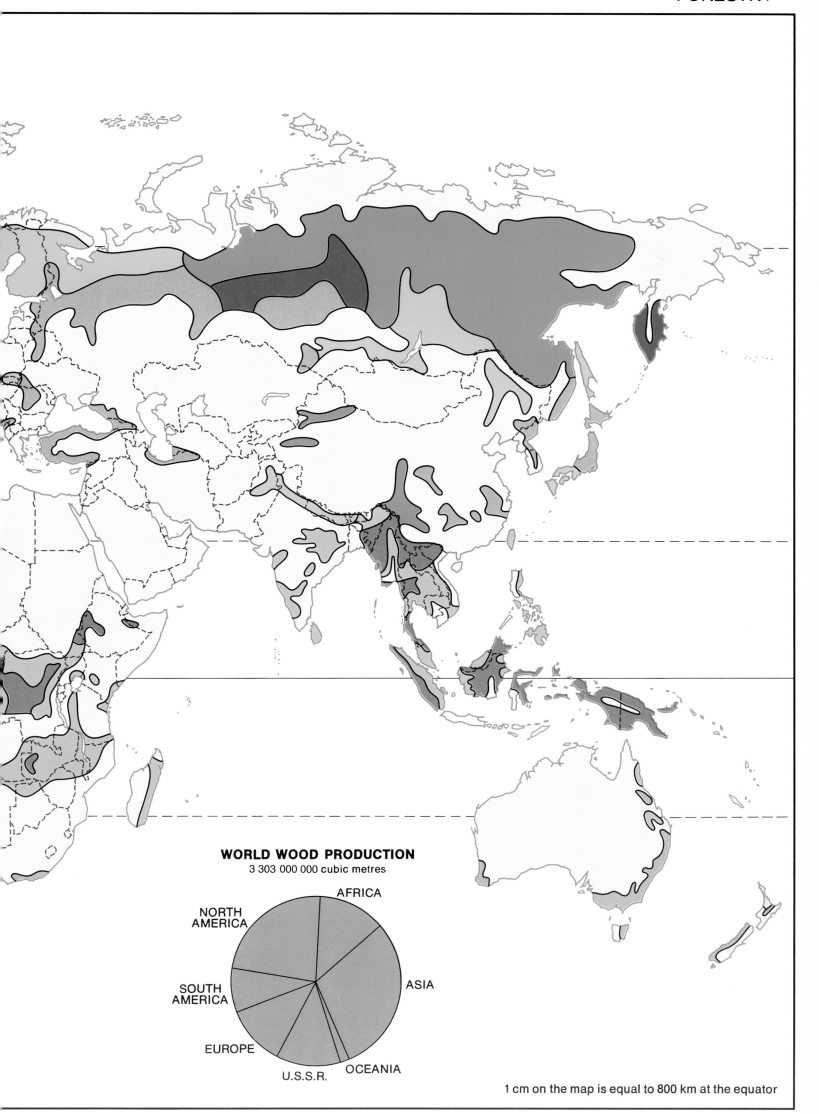

WORLD WOOD PRODUCTION
3 303 000 000 cubic metres

AFRICA

NORTH
AMERICA

ASIA

SOUTH
AMERICA

EUROPE

OCEANIA

U.S.S.R.

1 cm on the map is equal to 800 km at the equator

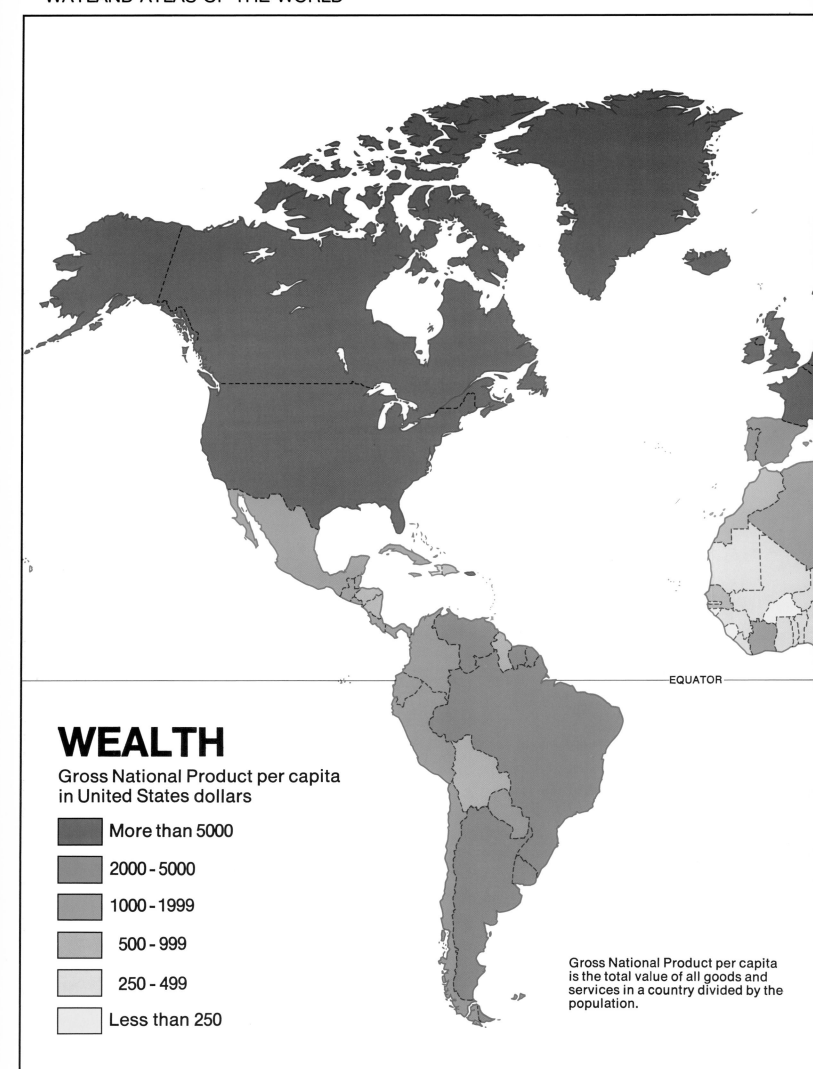

WEALTH

Gross National Product per capita
in United States dollars

More than 5000

2000 - 5000

1000 - 1999

500 - 999

250 - 499

Less than 250

EQUATOR

Gross National Product per capita
is the total value of all goods and
services in a country divided by the
population.

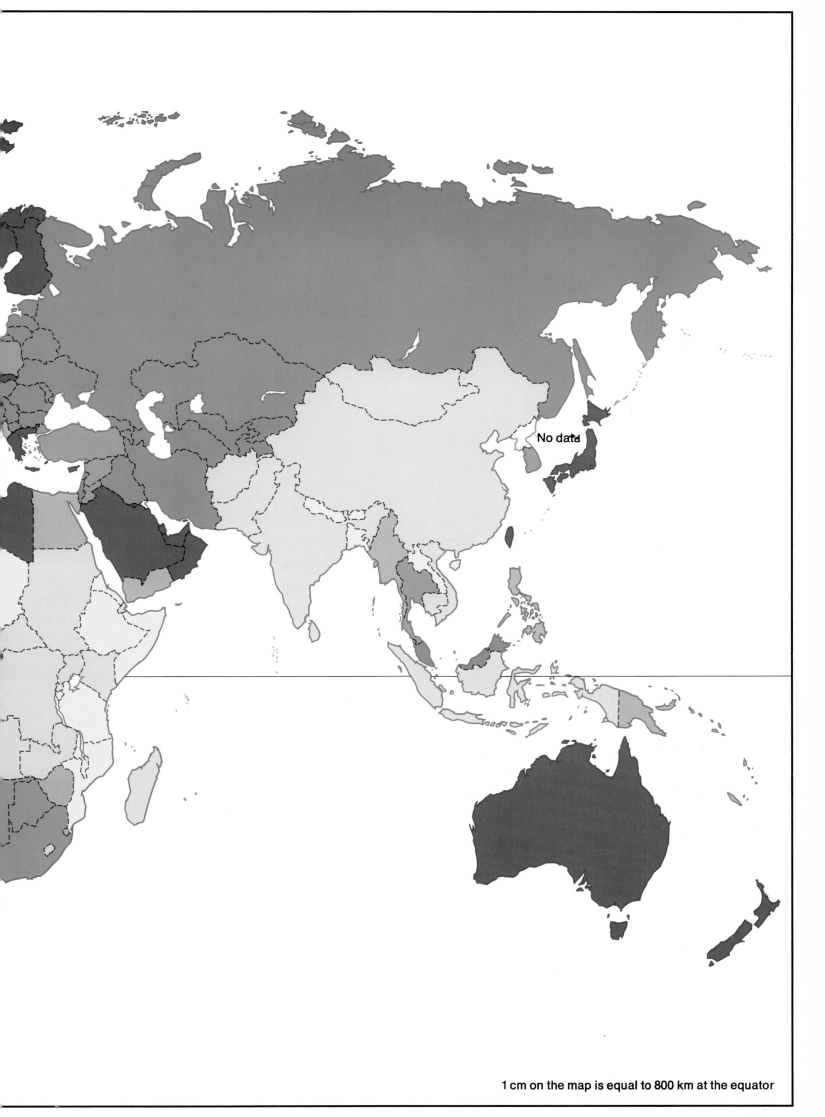

No data

1 cm on the map is equal to 800 km at the equator

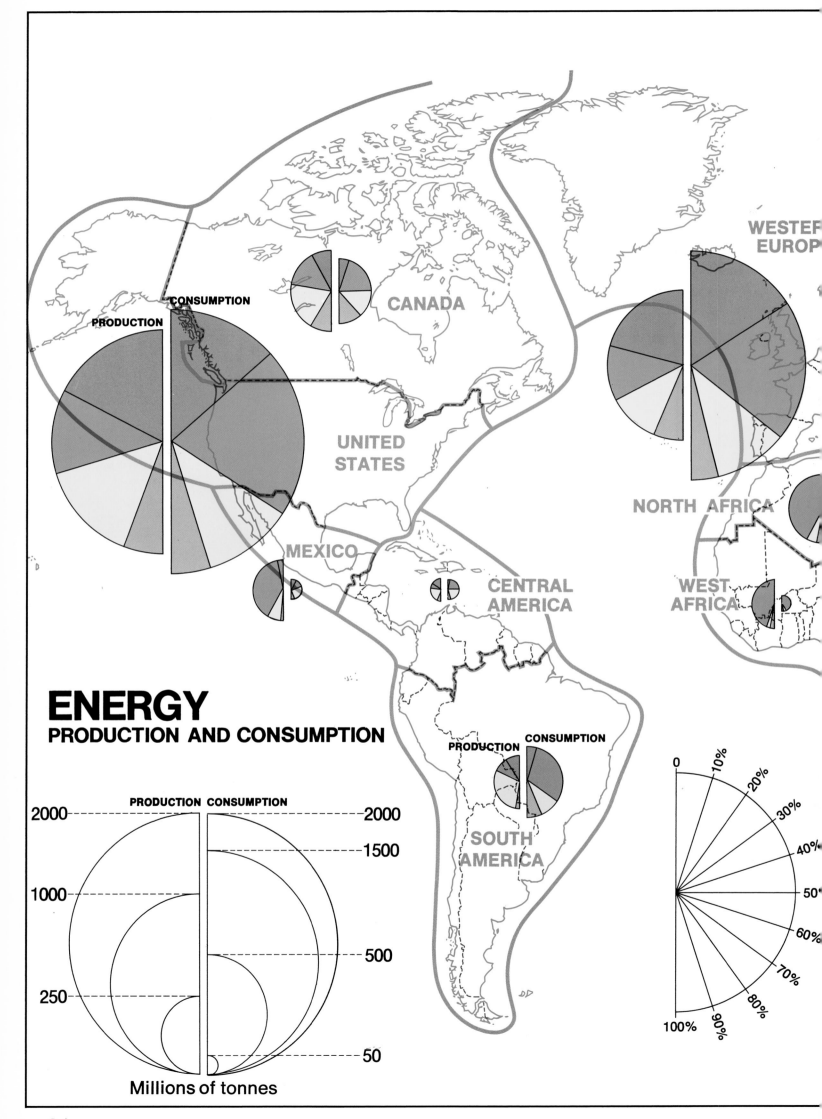

ENERGY
PRODUCTION AND CONSUMPTION

CANADA

UNITED
STATES

PRODUCTION   CONSUMPTION

MEXICO

CENTRAL
AMERICA

WESTERN
EUROPE

NORTH AFRICA

WEST
AFRICA

PRODUCTION   CONSUMPTION

SOUTH
AMERICA

PRODUCTION CONSUMPTION

2000 ----   ---- 2000
                         ---- 1500
1000 ----
                         ---- 500
250 ----
                         ---- 50

Millions of tonnes

0
10%
20%
30%
40%
50%
60%
70%
80%
90%
100%

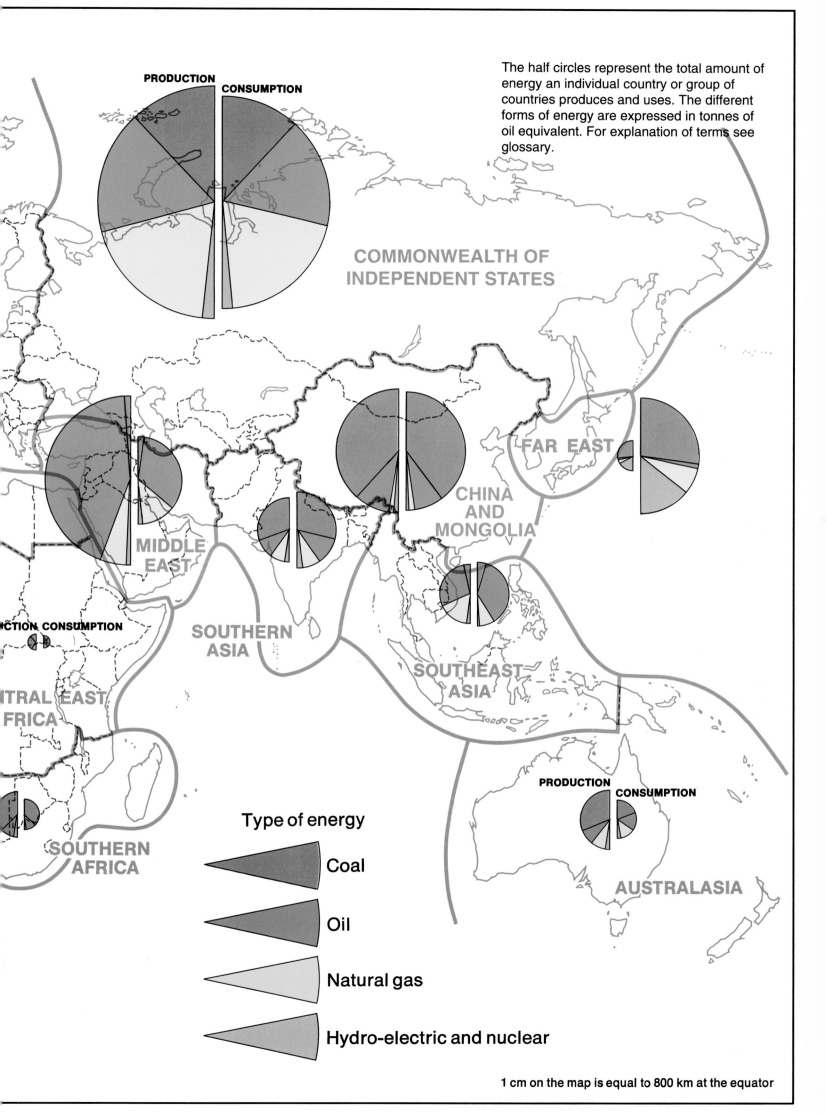

The half circles represent the total amount of energy an individual country or group of countries produces and uses. The different forms of energy are expressed in tonnes of oil equivalent. For explanation of terms see glossary.

PRODUCTION CONSUMPTION

COMMONWEALTH OF
INDEPENDENT STATES

FAR EAST

CHINA
AND
MONGOLIA

MIDDLE
EAST

...CTION CONSUMPTION

SOUTHERN
ASIA

...TRAL EAST
...FRICA

SOUTHEAST
ASIA

SOUTHERN
AFRICA

PRODUCTION CONSUMPTION

Type of energy

Coal

Oil

Natural gas

Hydro-electric and nuclear

AUSTRALASIA

1 cm on the map is equal to 800 km at the equator

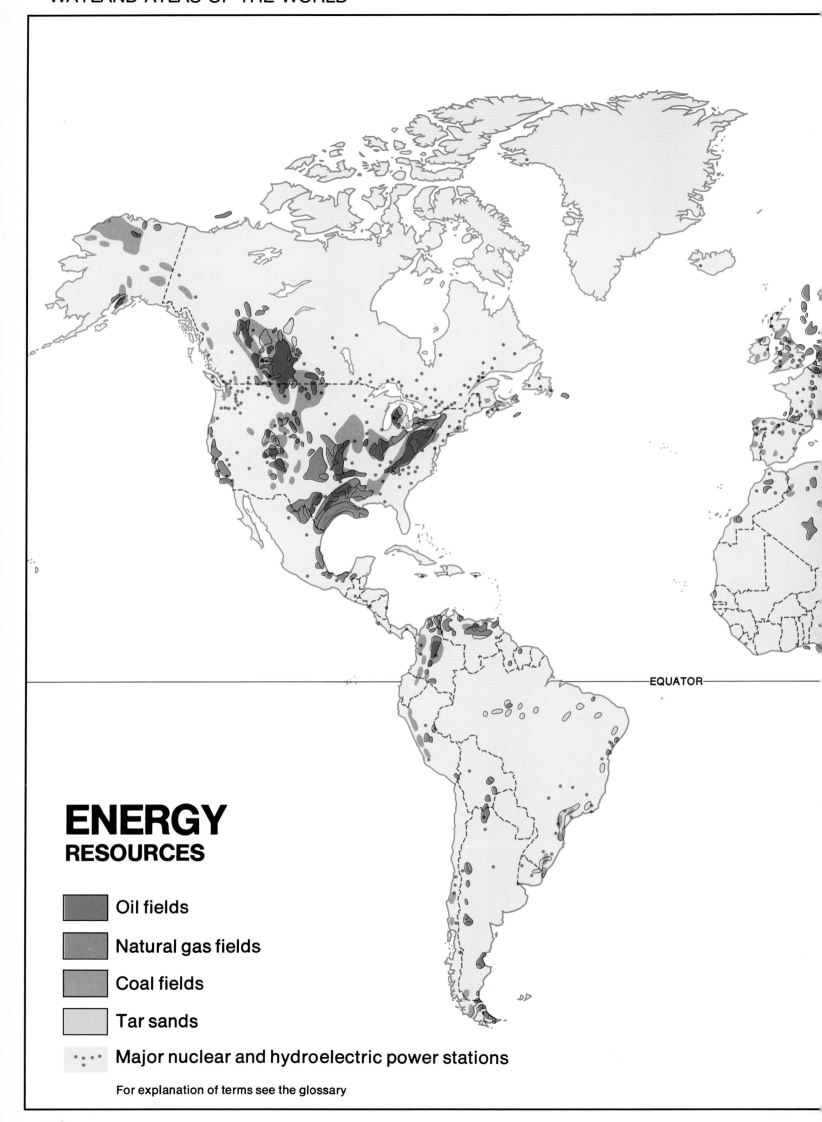

ENERGY
RESOURCES

Oil fields

Natural gas fields

Coal fields

Tar sands

Major nuclear and hydroelectric power stations

For explanation of terms see the glossary

EQUATOR

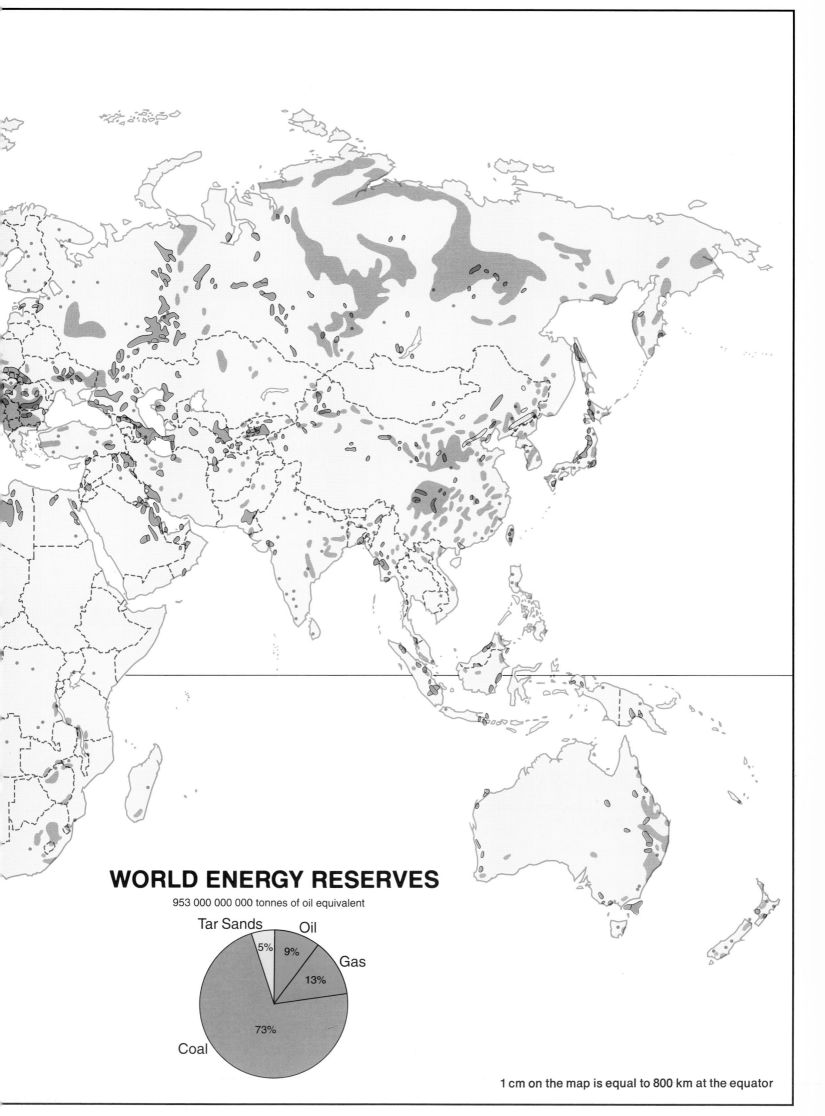

WORLD ENERGY RESERVES

953 000 000 000 tonnes of oil equivalent

Tar Sands

Oil

5%

9%

Gas

13%

73%

Coal

1 cm on the map is equal to 800 km at the equator

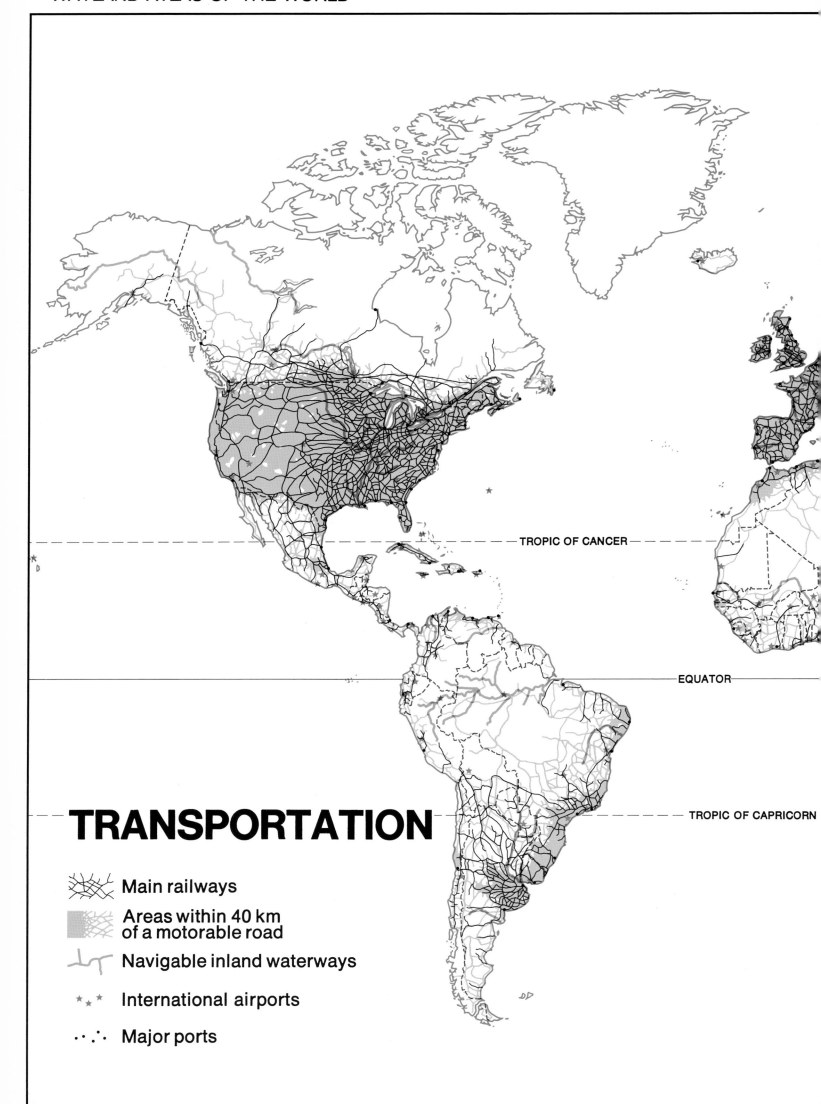

TROPIC OF CANCER

EQUATOR

TROPIC OF CAPRICORN

TRANSPORTATION

Main railways

Areas within 40 km
of a motorable road

Navigable inland waterways

International airports

Major ports

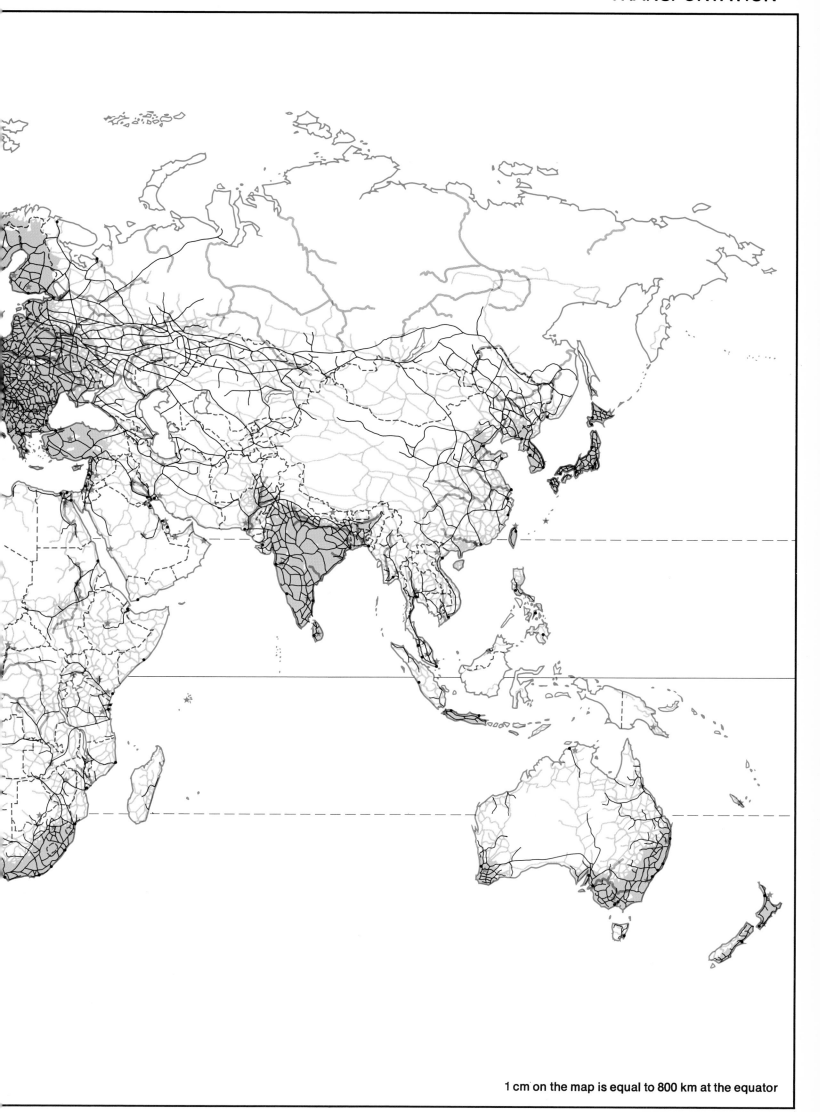

1 cm on the map is equal to 800 km at the equator

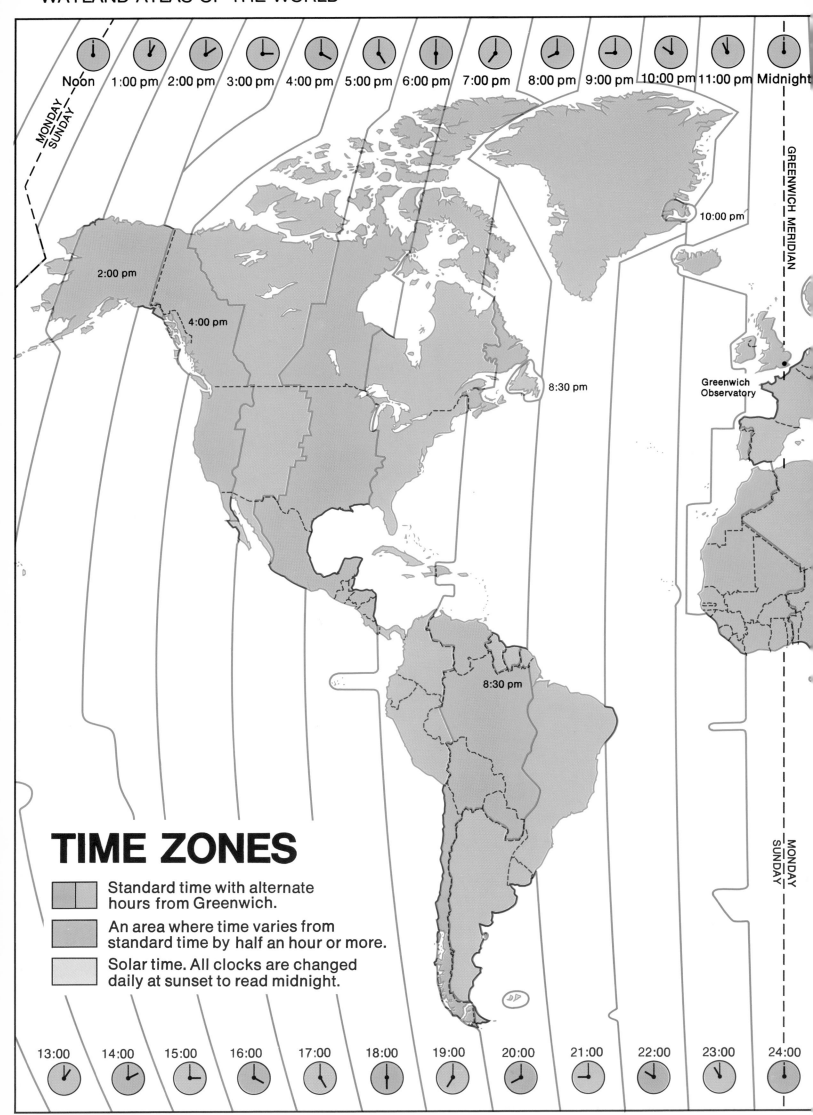

Noon | 1:00 pm | 2:00 pm | 3:00 pm | 4:00 pm | 5:00 pm | 6:00 pm | 7:00 pm | 8:00 pm | 9:00 pm | 10:00 pm | 11:00 pm | Midnight

MONDAY / SUNDAY

GREENWICH MERIDIAN

2:00 pm

4:00 pm

10:00 pm

8:30 pm

Greenwich
Observatory

8:30 pm

TIME ZONES

Standard time with alternate
hours from Greenwich.

An area where time varies from
standard time by half an hour or more.

Solar time. All clocks are changed
daily at sunset to read midnight.

MONDAY / SUNDAY

13:00 | 14:00 | 15:00 | 16:00 | 17:00 | 18:00 | 19:00 | 20:00 | 21:00 | 22:00 | 23:00 | 24:00

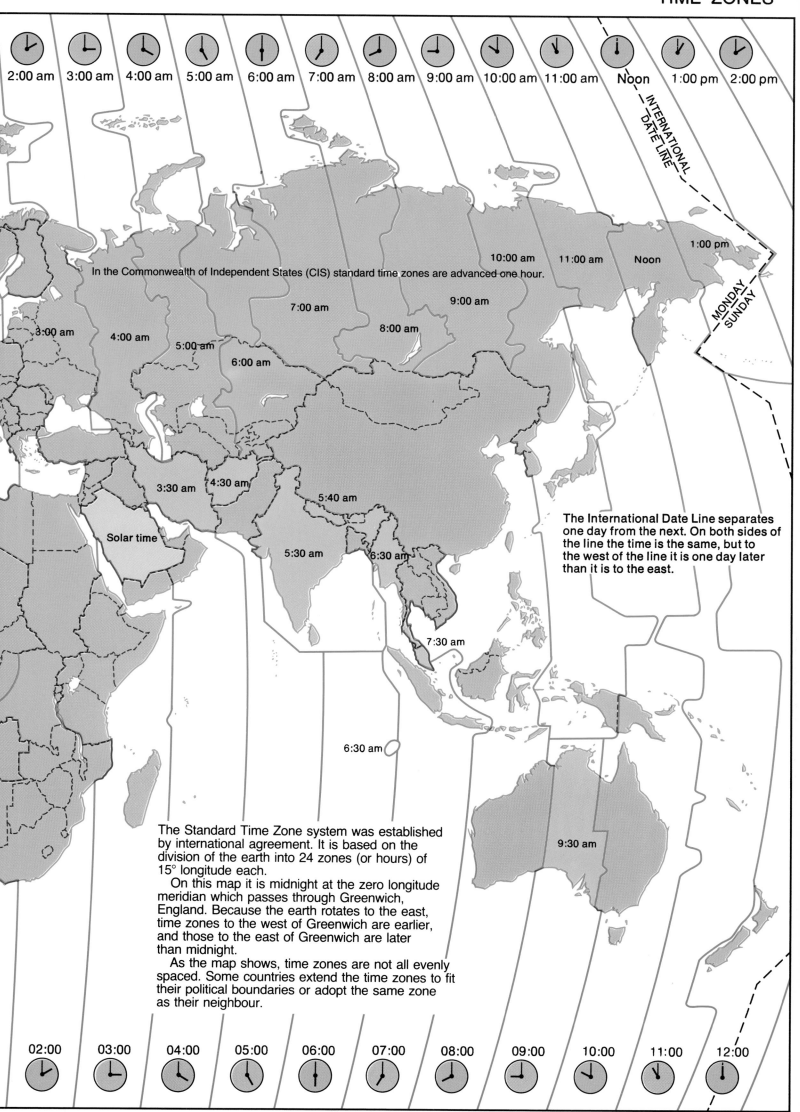

2:00 am 3:00 am 4:00 am 5:00 am 6:00 am 7:00 am 8:00 am 9:00 am 10:00 am 11:00 am Noon 1:00 pm 2:00 pm

INTERNATIONAL DATE LINE

In the Commonwealth of Independent States (CIS) standard time zones are advanced one hour.

10:00 am 11:00 am Noon 1:00 pm

9:00 am

7:00 am 8:00 am

3:00 am 4:00 am 5:00 am

6:00 am

MONDAY / SUNDAY

3:30 am 4:30 am

5:40 am

Solar time

The International Date Line separates one day from the next. On both sides of the line the time is the same, but to the west of the line it is one day later than it is to the east.

5:30 am 6:30 am

7:30 am

6:30 am

9:30 am

The Standard Time Zone system was established by international agreement. It is based on the division of the earth into 24 zones (or hours) of 15° longitude each.

On this map it is midnight at the zero longitude meridian which passes through Greenwich, England. Because the earth rotates to the east, time zones to the west of Greenwich are earlier, and those to the east of Greenwich are later than midnight.

As the map shows, time zones are not all evenly spaced. Some countries extend the time zones to fit their political boundaries or adopt the same zone as their neighbour.

02:00 03:00 04:00 05:00 06:00 07:00 08:00 09:00 10:00 11:00 12:00

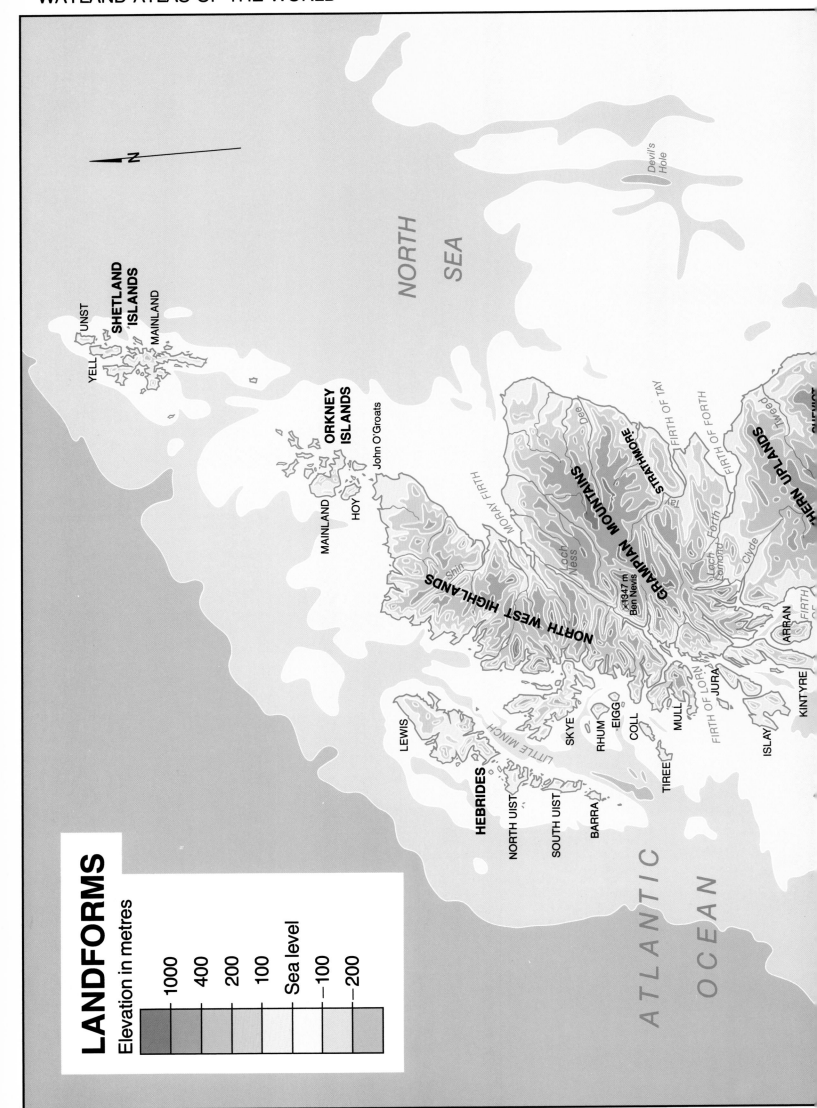

N

SHETLAND ISLANDS

UNST

YELL

MAINLAND

NORTH SEA

Devil's Hole

ORKNEY ISLANDS

MAINLAND

HOY

John O'Groats

MORAY FIRTH

Shin

Dee

FIRTH OF TAY

FIRTH OF FORTH

STRATHMORE

GRAMPIAN MOUNTAINS

NORTH WEST HIGHLANDS

Loch Ness

Tay

Forth

Loch Lomond

Clyde

×1347 m
Ben Nevis

Tweed

HERN UPLANDS

ARRAN

FIRTH OF

FIRTH OF LORN

JURA

MULL

KINTYRE

ISLAY

LEWIS

LITTLE MINCH

SKYE

RHUM

EIGG

COLL

TIREE

HEBRIDES

NORTH UIST

SOUTH UIST

BARRA

ATLANTIC OCEAN

LANDFORMS

Elevation in metres

1000
400
200
100
Sea level
-100
-200

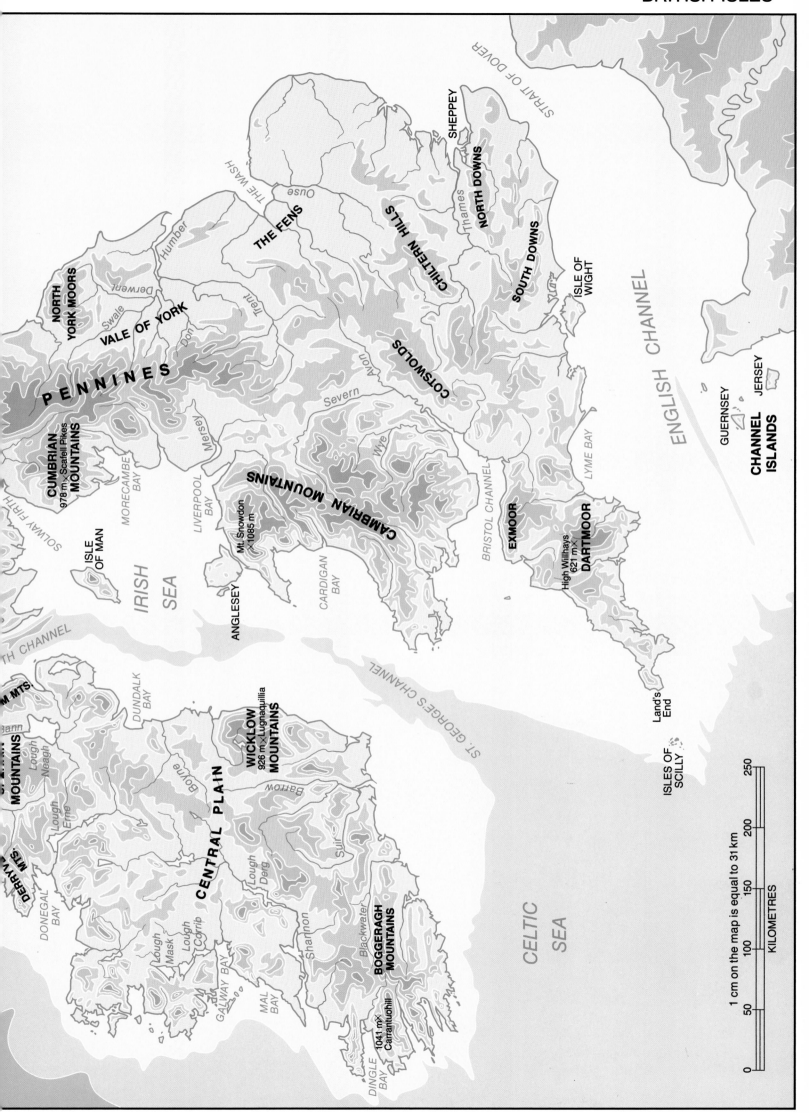

STRAIT OF DOVER

SHEPPEY

NORTH DOWNS

THE FENS

CHILTERN HILLS

Thames

Ouse

THE WASH

Humber

SOUTH DOWNS

ISLE OF WIGHT

Derwent

NORTH YORK MOORS

Swale

VALE OF YORK

Don

Trent

COTSWOLDS

ENGLISH CHANNEL

P E N N I N E S

Avon

Severn

Mersey

Wye

JERSEY

GUERNSEY

CUMBRIAN
978 m ×Scafell Pikes
MOUNTAINS

CAMBRIAN MOUNTAINS

CHANNEL ISLANDS

MORECAMBE BAY

BRISTOL CHANNEL

LYME BAY

EXMOOR

SOLWAY FIRTH

ISLE OF MAN

Mt. Snowdon
×1085 m

LIVERPOOL BAY

DARTMOOR
High Willhays
621 m×

IRISH SEA

ANGLESEY

CARDIGAN BAY

TH CHANNEL

Land's
End

M. MTS.

DUNDALK BAY

WICKLOW
926 m×Lugnaquillia
MOUNTAINS

ST. GEORGE'S CHANNEL

Bann

MOUNTAINS

Lough
Neagh

Boyne

CENTRAL PLAIN

Barrow

ISLES OF SCILLY

Lough
Erne

DERRY MTS.

Suir

Lough
Derg

CELTIC SEA

DONEGAL BAY

Lough
Corrib

Shannon

Lough
Mask

Blackwater

BOGGERAGH MOUNTAINS

GALWAY BAY

MAL BAY

DINGLE BAY

1041 m×
Carrantuohill

1 cm on the map is equal to 31 km

0   50   100   150   200   250

KILOMETRES

33

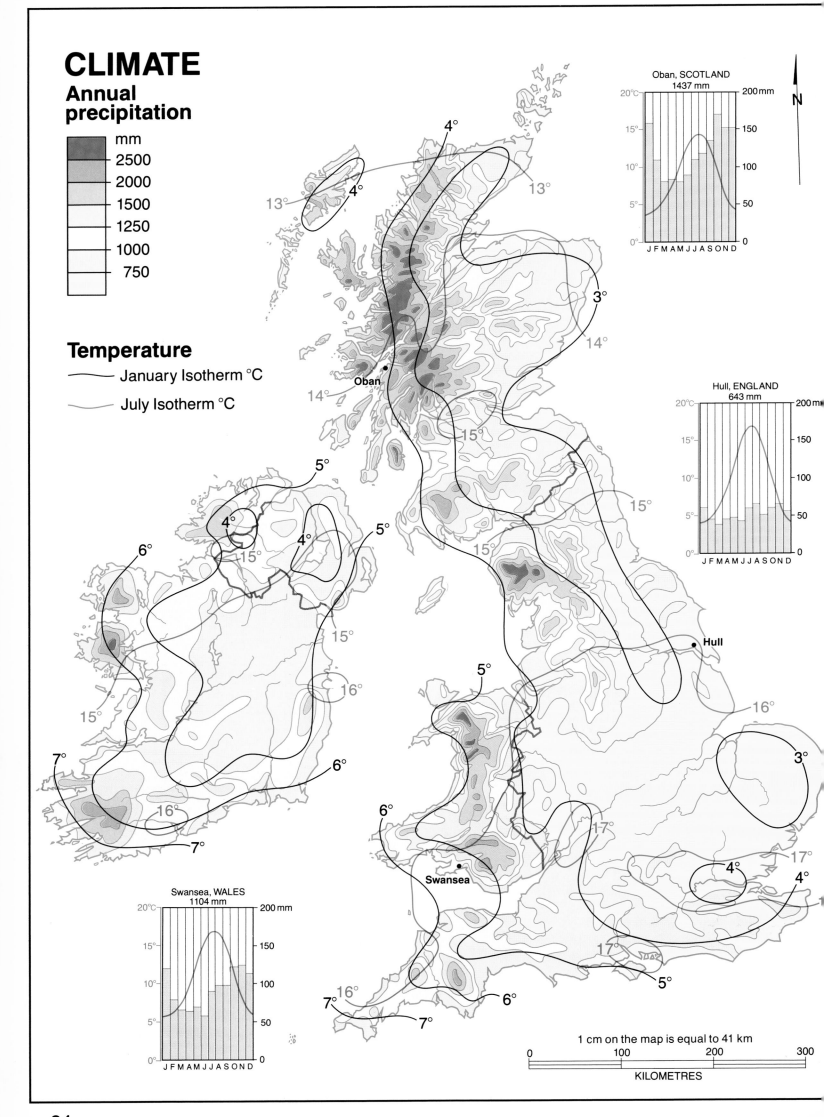

CLIMATE

Annual precipitation

	mm
	2500
	2000
	1500
	1250
	1000
	750

Temperature

—— January Isotherm °C

—— July Isotherm °C

Oban, SCOTLAND
1437 mm

Hull, ENGLAND
643 mm

Swansea, WALES
1104 mm

1 cm on the map is equal to 41 km

0   100   200   300

KILOMETRES

FARMING

1	Intensive farming
2	Mainly grain farming
3	Mixed farming
4	Mainly dairy farming
5	Livestock and grazing
	No farming
	Built-up areas
	National boundary

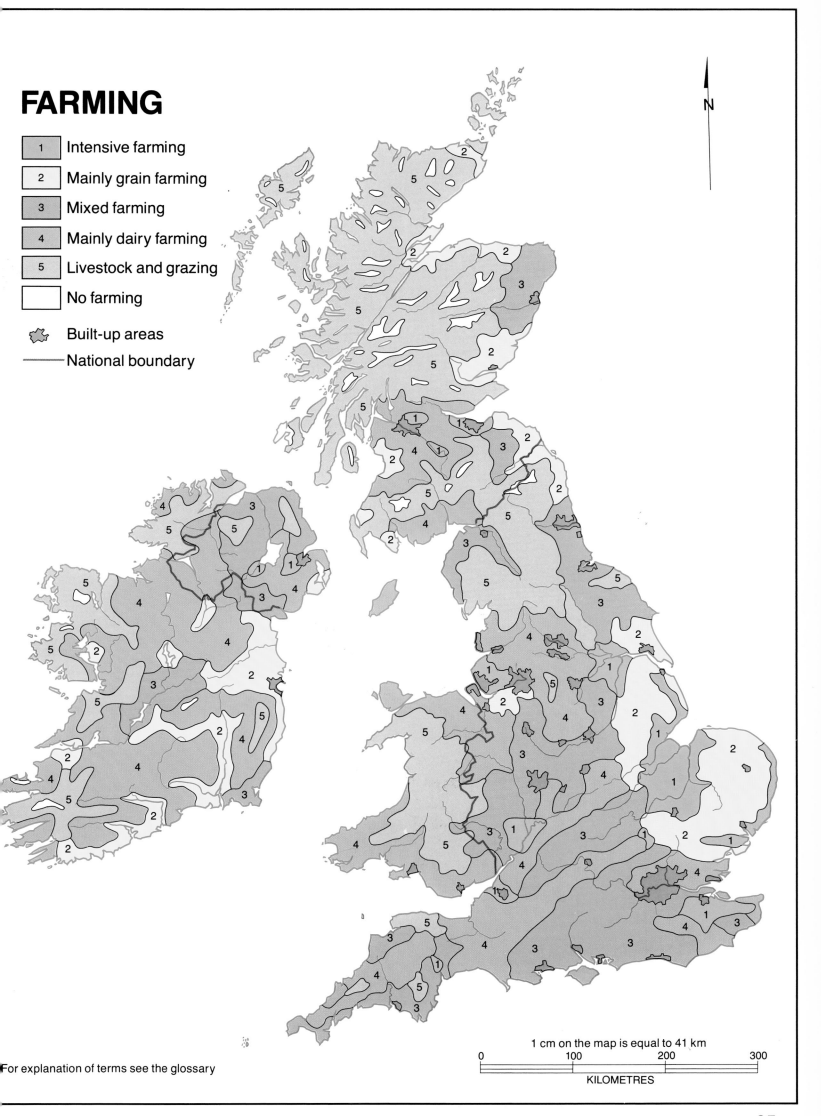

N

1 cm on the map is equal to 41 km

0   100   200   300

KILOMETRES

For explanation of terms see the glossary

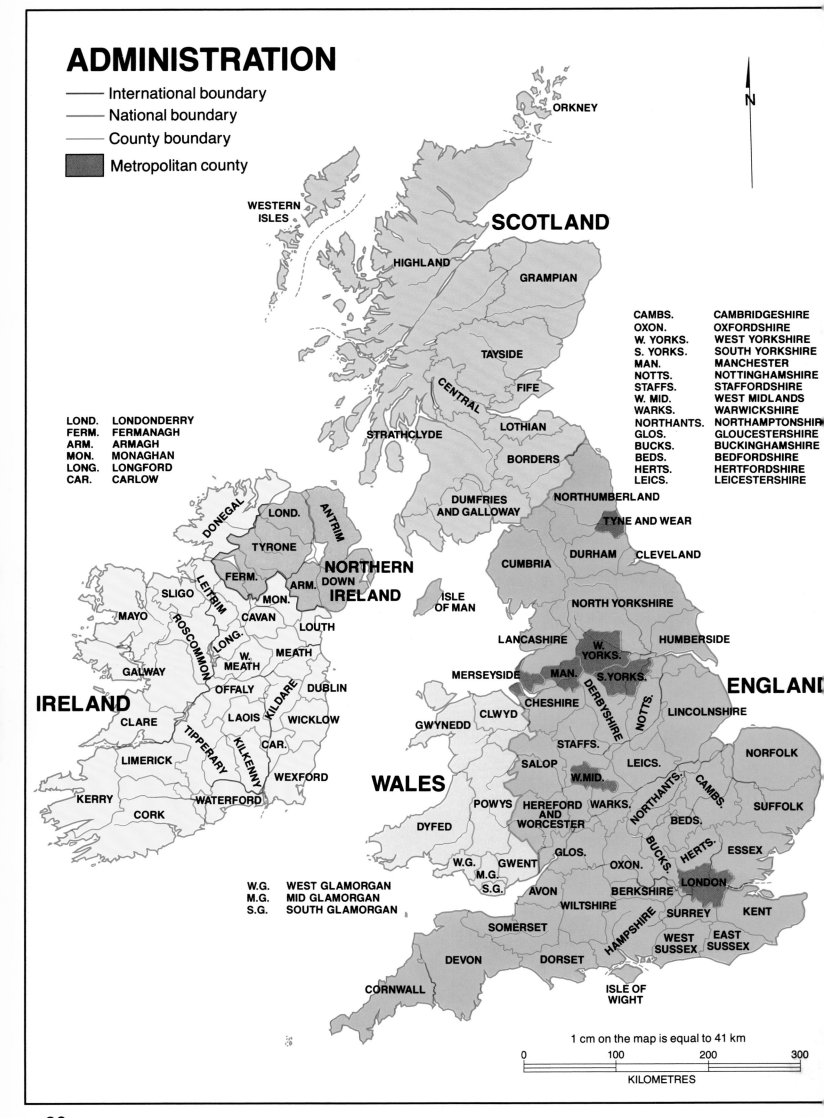

ADMINISTRATION

—————— International boundary
——————— National boundary
——————— County boundary
Metropolitan county

CAMBS.	CAMBRIDGESHIRE
OXON.	OXFORDSHIRE
W. YORKS.	WEST YORKSHIRE
S. YORKS.	SOUTH YORKSHIRE
MAN.	MANCHESTER
NOTTS.	NOTTINGHAMSHIRE
STAFFS.	STAFFORDSHIRE
W. MID.	WEST MIDLANDS
WARKS.	WARWICKSHIRE
NORTHANTS.	NORTHAMPTONSHIRE
GLOS.	GLOUCESTERSHIRE
BUCKS.	BUCKINGHAMSHIRE
BEDS.	BEDFORDSHIRE
HERTS.	HERTFORDSHIRE
LEICS.	LEICESTERSHIRE

LOND.	LONDONDERRY
FERM.	FERMANAGH
ARM.	ARMAGH
MON.	MONAGHAN
LONG.	LONGFORD
CAR.	CARLOW

ORKNEY

N

WESTERN ISLES

SCOTLAND

HIGHLAND

GRAMPIAN

TAYSIDE

CENTRAL

FIFE

STRATHCLYDE

LOTHIAN

BORDERS

DUMFRIES AND GALLOWAY

NORTHUMBERLAND

TYNE AND WEAR

DURHAM   CLEVELAND

CUMBRIA

ISLE OF MAN

NORTH YORKSHIRE

HUMBERSIDE

LANCASHIRE

W. YORKS.

MERSEYSIDE

MAN.   S.YORKS.

CHESHIRE

DERBYSHIRE

NOTTS.

LINCOLNSHIRE

ENGLAND

DONEGAL

LOND.   ANTRIM

TYRONE

NORTHERN

FERM.

ARM.   DOWN

IRELAND

SLIGO

LEITRIM

MON.

MAYO

ROSCOMMON

LONG.

CAVAN

LOUTH

W. MEATH

MEATH

GALWAY

OFFALY

DUBLIN

IRELAND

CLARE

LAOIS

KILDARE

WICKLOW

TIPPERARY

KILKENNY

CAR.

LIMERICK

WEXFORD

KERRY

WATERFORD

CORK

WALES

GWYNEDD

CLWYD

STAFFS.

SALOP

W.MID.

POWYS

HEREFORD AND WORCESTER

WARKS.

NORTHANTS.

CAMBS.

NORFOLK

DYFED

BEDS.

SUFFOLK

W.G.   GWENT

GLOS.

BUCKS.

HERTS.

ESSEX

M.G.

OXON.

S.G.

AVON

BERKSHIRE

LONDON

W.G.   WEST GLAMORGAN
M.G.   MID GLAMORGAN
S.G.   SOUTH GLAMORGAN

WILTSHIRE

HAMPSHIRE

SURREY

KENT

SOMERSET

DORSET

WEST SUSSEX

EAST SUSSEX

DEVON

ISLE OF WIGHT

CORNWALL

1 cm on the map is equal to 41 km

0   100   200   300

KILOMETRES

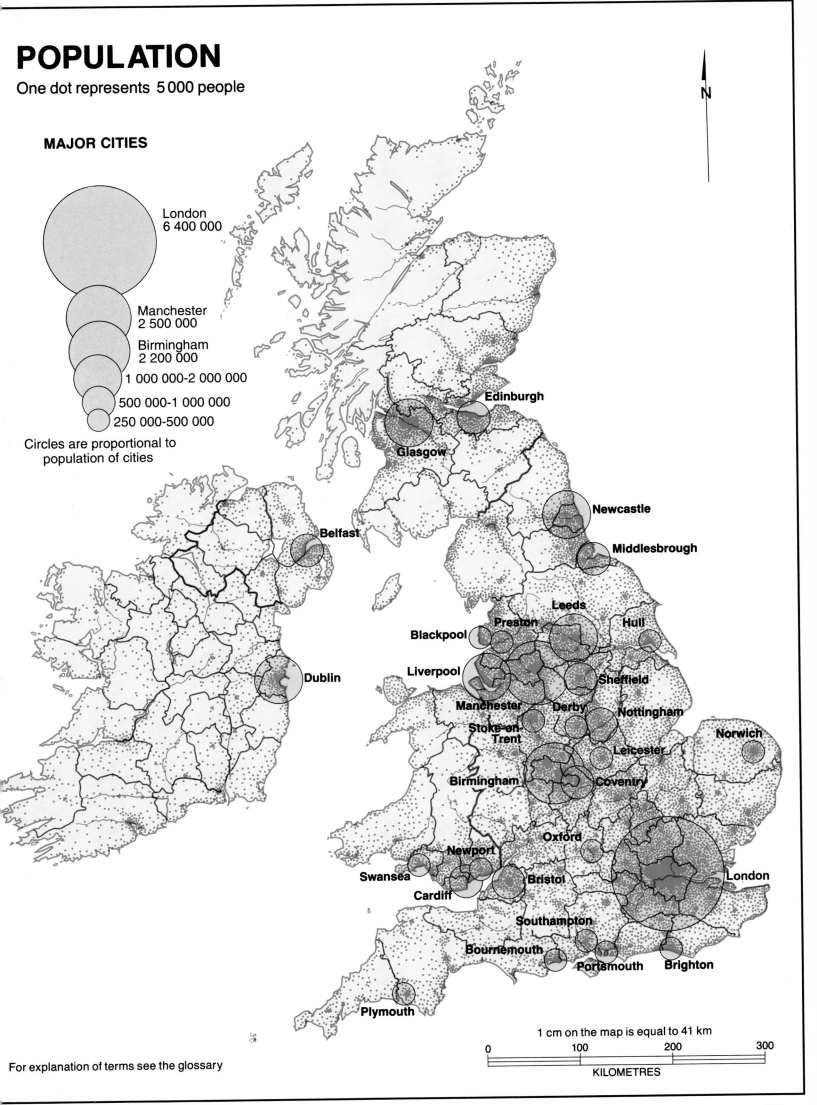

POPULATION

One dot represents 5 000 people

MAJOR CITIES

London
6 400 000

Manchester
2 500 000

Birmingham
2 200 000

1 000 000-2 000 000

500 000-1 000 000

250 000-500 000

Circles are proportional to
population of cities

N

Edinburgh

Glasgow

Belfast

Newcastle

Middlesbrough

Dublin

Leeds

Preston

Blackpool

Hull

Liverpool

Sheffield

Manchester

Derby

Nottingham

Stoke-on-Trent

Norwich

Birmingham

Leicester

Coventry

Oxford

Newport

Swansea

Bristol

London

Cardiff

Southampton

Bournemouth

Portsmouth

Brighton

Plymouth

1 cm on the map is equal to 41 km

0   100   200   300

KILOMETRES

For explanation of terms see the glossary

37

MINERALS

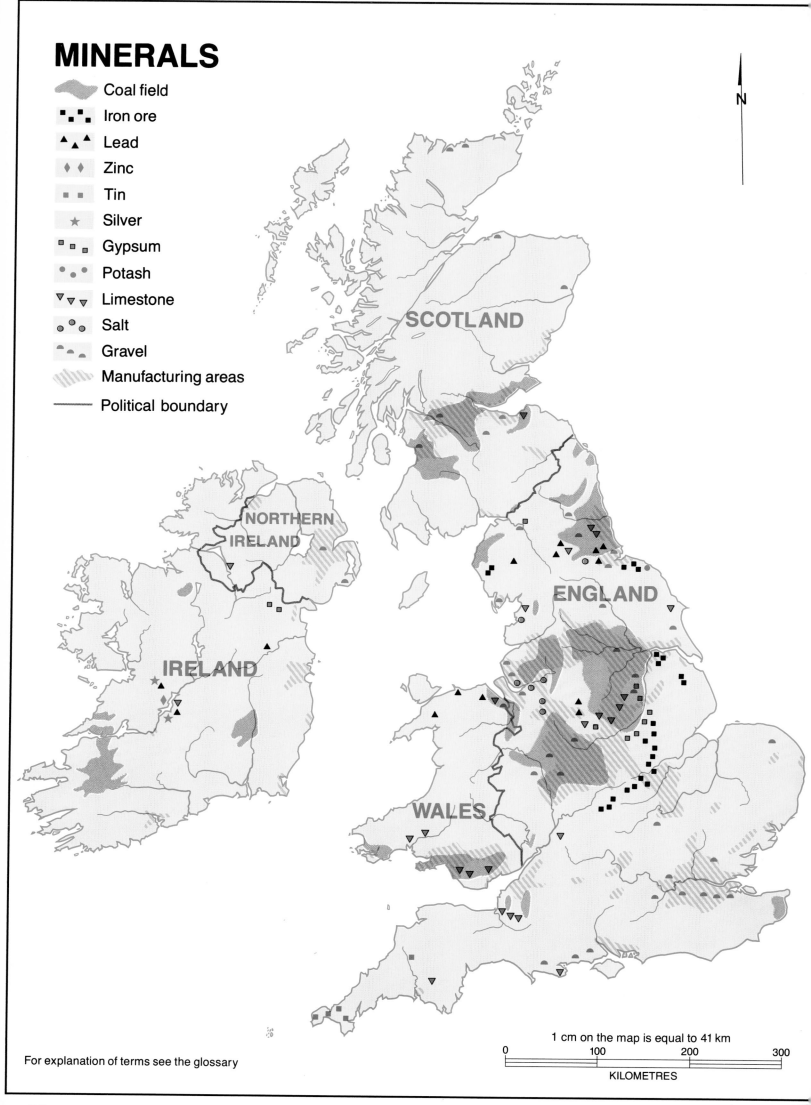

Coal field

Iron ore

Lead

Zinc

Tin

Silver

Gypsum

Potash

Limestone

Salt

Gravel

Manufacturing areas

Political boundary

SCOTLAND

NORTHERN IRELAND

IRELAND

ENGLAND

WALES

1 cm on the map is equal to 41 km

0   100   200   300

KILOMETRES

For explanation of terms see the glossary

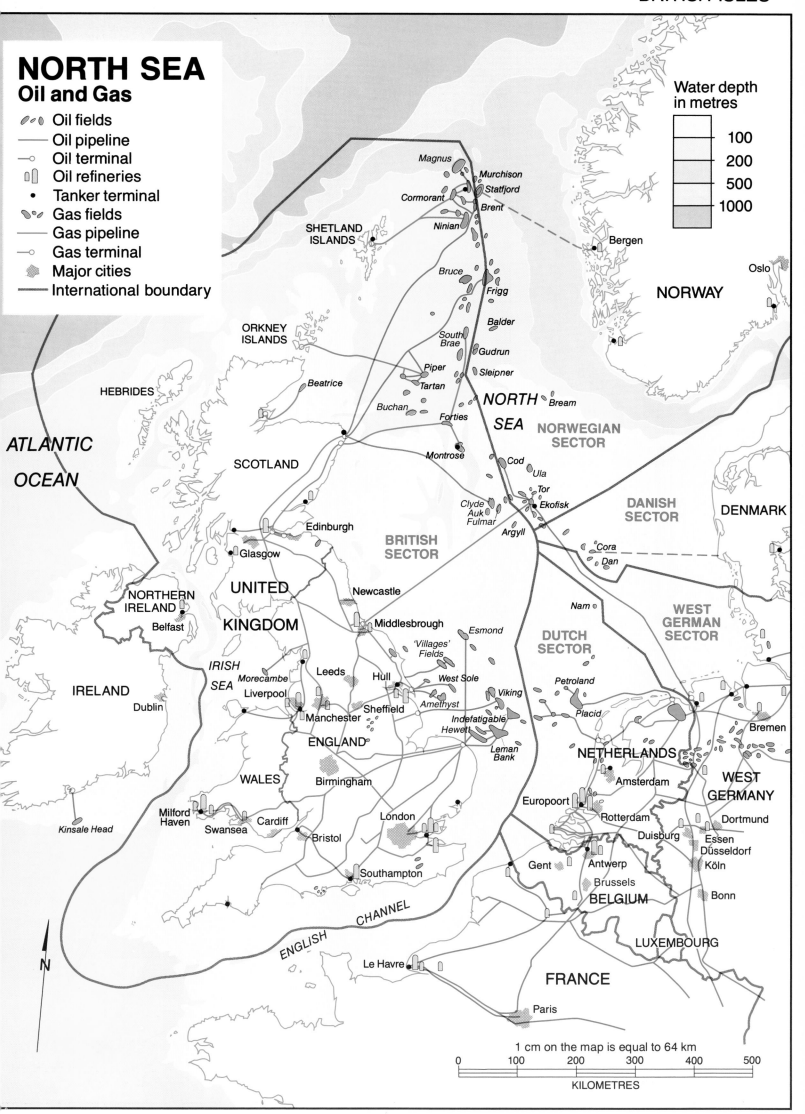

NORTH SEA
Oil and Gas

- Oil fields
- Oil pipeline
- Oil terminal
- Oil refineries
- Tanker terminal
- Gas fields
- Gas pipeline
- Gas terminal
- Major cities
- International boundary

Water depth
in metres

100
200
500
1000

ATLANTIC

OCEAN

Magnus
Murchison
Statfjord
Cormorant
Brent
Ninian

SHETLAND
ISLANDS

Bergen

NORWAY

Oslo

Bruce
Frigg
Balder
South
Brae
Gudrun
Sleipner

ORKNEY
ISLANDS

HEBRIDES

Beatrice

Piper
Tartan
Buchan
Forties

NORTH
SEA

Bream

NORWEGIAN
SECTOR

SCOTLAND

Montrose

Cod
Ula
Tor
Clyde
Auk
Fulmar
Ekofisk
Argyll

DANISH
SECTOR

DENMARK

Edinburgh

Glasgow

Cora
Dan

BRITISH
SECTOR

UNITED

Newcastle

Nam

WEST
GERMAN
SECTOR

NORTHERN
IRELAND

Belfast

KINGDOM

Middlesbrough

'Villages'
Fields

Esmond

DUTCH
SECTOR

IRISH
SEA

Morecambe
Liverpool

Leeds

Hull
West Sole

Viking

Petroland

Bremen

IRELAND

Dublin

Manchester
Sheffield

Amethyst

Indefatigable
Hewett

Placid

ENGLAND

Leman
Bank

NETHERLANDS

WEST
GERMANY

Dortmund

WALES

Birmingham

Amsterdam

Rotterdam

Duisburg

Essen
Düsseldorf
Köln

Milford
Haven
Swansea
Cardiff

London

Europoort

Gent
Antwerp

Bonn

Kinsale Head

Bristol

Southampton

Brussels
BELGIUM

LUXEMBOURG

N

ENGLISH CHANNEL

Le Havre

FRANCE

Paris

1 cm on the map is equal to 64 km

0   100   200   300   400   500

KILOMETRES

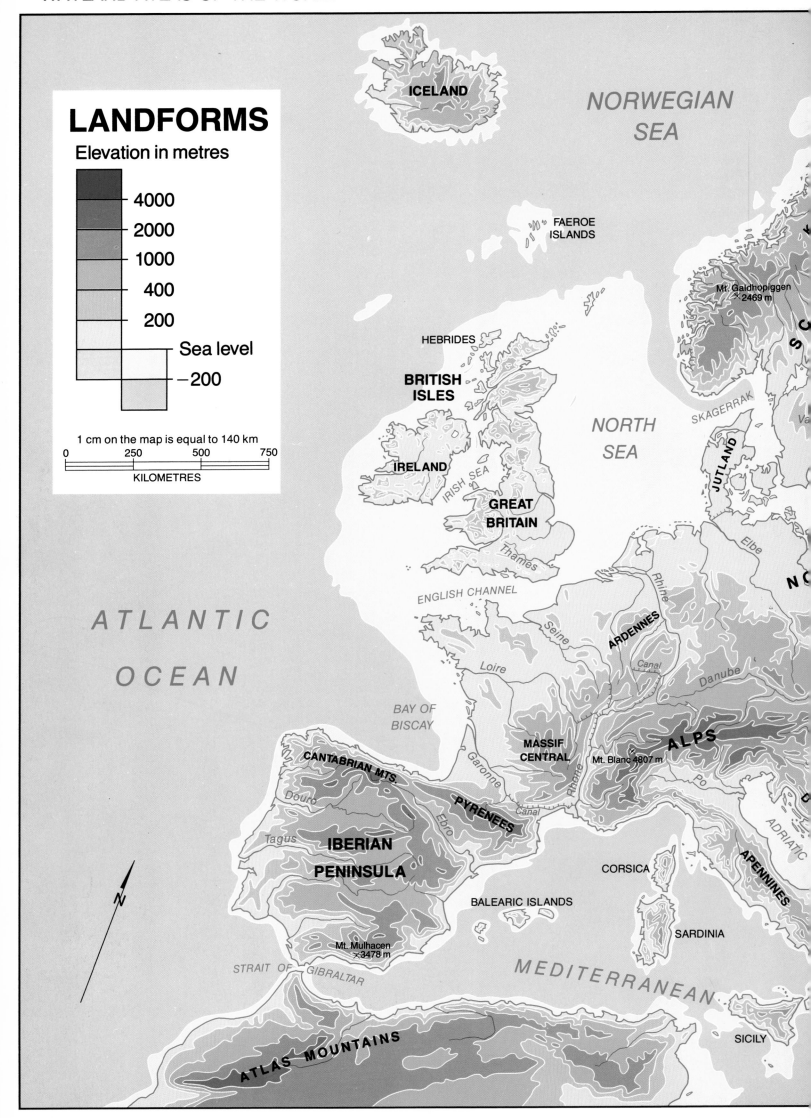

LANDFORMS

Elevation in metres

4000
2000
1000
400
200
Sea level
200

1 cm on the map is equal to 140 km

0   250   500   750
KILOMETRES

ICELAND

NORWEGIAN SEA

FAEROE ISLANDS

HEBRIDES

BRITISH ISLES

NORTH SEA

Mt. Galdhopiggen ✕ 2469 m

SKAGERRAK

JUTLAND

IRELAND

IRISH SEA

GREAT BRITAIN

Thames

Elbe

Rhine

ENGLISH CHANNEL

ATLANTIC OCEAN

Seine

Loire

ARDENNES

Canal

Danube

BAY OF BISCAY

Garonne

MASSIF CENTRAL

Mt. Blanc 4807 m

ALPS

Po

CANTABRIAN MTS.

Rhone

Douro

PYRENEES

Canal

Ebro

ADRIATIC

APENNINES

Tagus

IBERIAN PENINSULA

CORSICA

BALEARIC ISLANDS

SARDINIA

Mt. Mulhacen ✕ 3478 m

MEDITERRANEAN

STRAIT OF GIBRALTAR

SICILY

ATLAS MOUNTAINS

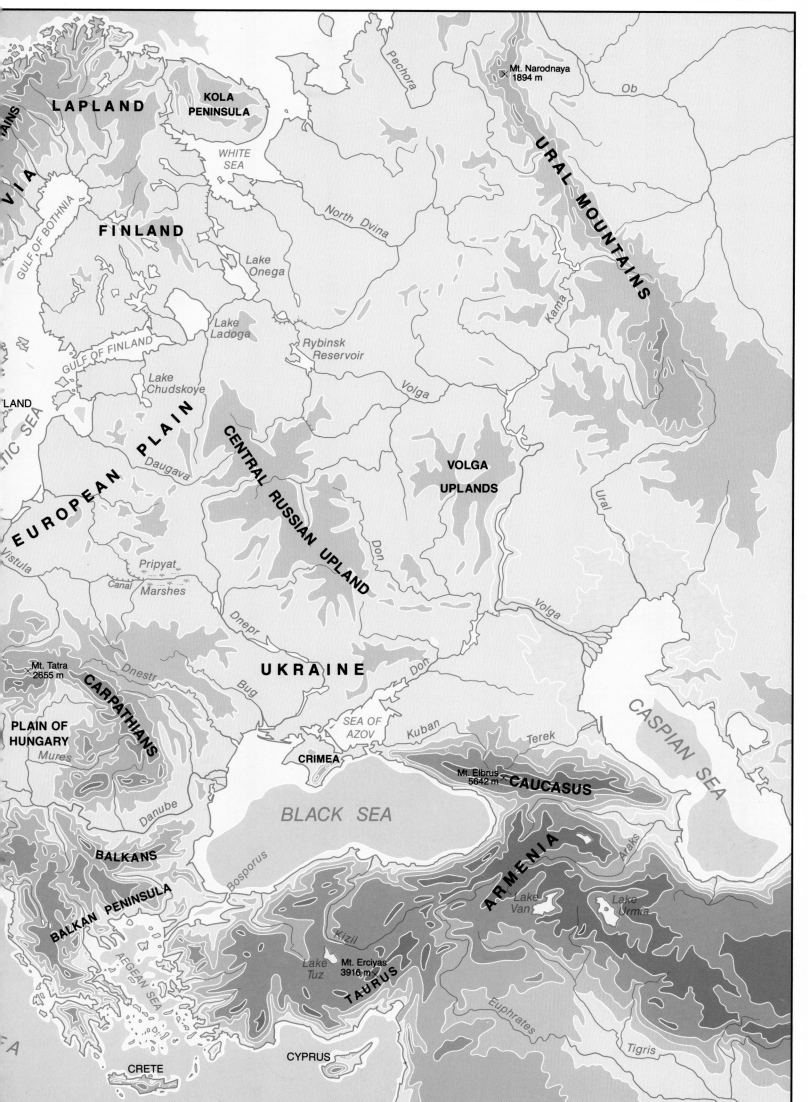

LAPLAND

KOLA
PENINSULA

VIA

FINLAND

WHITE
SEA

Pechora

Mt. Narodnaya
1894 m

Ob

URAL MOUNTAINS

GULF OF BOTHNIA

North Dvina

Lake
Onega

Kama

LAND

GULF OF FINLAND

Lake
Ladoga

Rybinsk
Reservoir

Volga

TIC SEA

EUROPEAN PLAIN

Lake
Chudskoye

Daugava

CENTRAL RUSSIAN UPLAND

VOLGA
UPLANDS

Ural

Vistula

Pripyat

Don

Volga

Canal

Marshes

Dnepr

UKRAINE

Don

CASPIAN SEA

Mt. Tatra
2655 m

Dnestr

Bug

SEA OF
AZOV

Kuban

Terek

CARPATHIANS

PLAIN OF
HUNGARY

Mures

CRIMEA

Mt. Elbrus
5642 m

CAUCASUS

Danube

BLACK SEA

ARMENIA

Araks

BALKANS

Bosporus

Lake
Van

Lake
Urmia

BALKAN PENINSULA

AEGEAN SEA

Kizil

TAURUS

Lake
Tuz

Mt. Erciyas
3916 m

Euphrates

A

CRETE

CYPRUS

Tigris

41

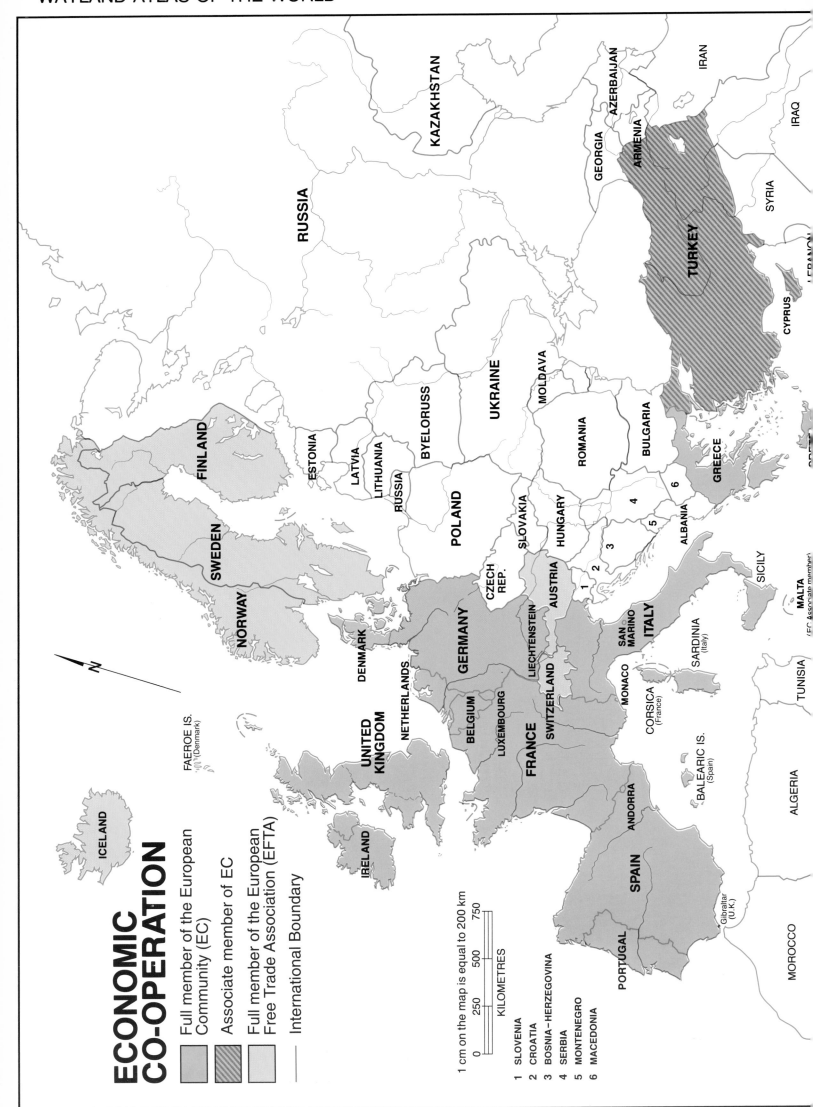

ECONOMIC CO-OPERATION

Full member of the European Community (EC)

Associate member of EC

Full member of the European Free Trade Association (EFTA)

International Boundary

1 cm on the map is equal to 200 km

0   250   500   750
KILOMETRES

1 SLOVENIA
2 CROATIA
3 BOSNIA–HERZEGOVINA
4 SERBIA
5 MONTENEGRO
6 MACEDONIA

N

ICELAND

FAEROE IS.
(Denmark)

UNITED KINGDOM

IRELAND

NETHERLANDS

BELGIUM

LUXEMBOURG

FRANCE

SWITZERLAND

LIECHTENSTEIN

GERMANY

DENMARK

CZECH REP.

AUSTRIA

MONACO

CORSICA (France)

SAN MARINO

ITALY

SARDINIA (Italy)

BALEARIC IS. (Spain)

ANDORRA

SPAIN

PORTUGAL

Gibraltar (U.K.)

NORWAY

SWEDEN

FINLAND

ESTONIA

LATVIA

LITHUANIA

RUSSIA

POLAND

SLOVAKIA

HUNGARY

BYELORUSS

UKRAINE

MOLDAVA

ROMANIA

BULGARIA

ALBANIA

GREECE

SICILY

MALTA
(EC Associate member)

TUNISIA

ALGERIA

MOROCCO

RUSSIA

KAZAKHSTAN

GEORGIA

ARMENIA

AZERBAIJAN

TURKEY

IRAN

IRAQ

SYRIA

CYPRUS

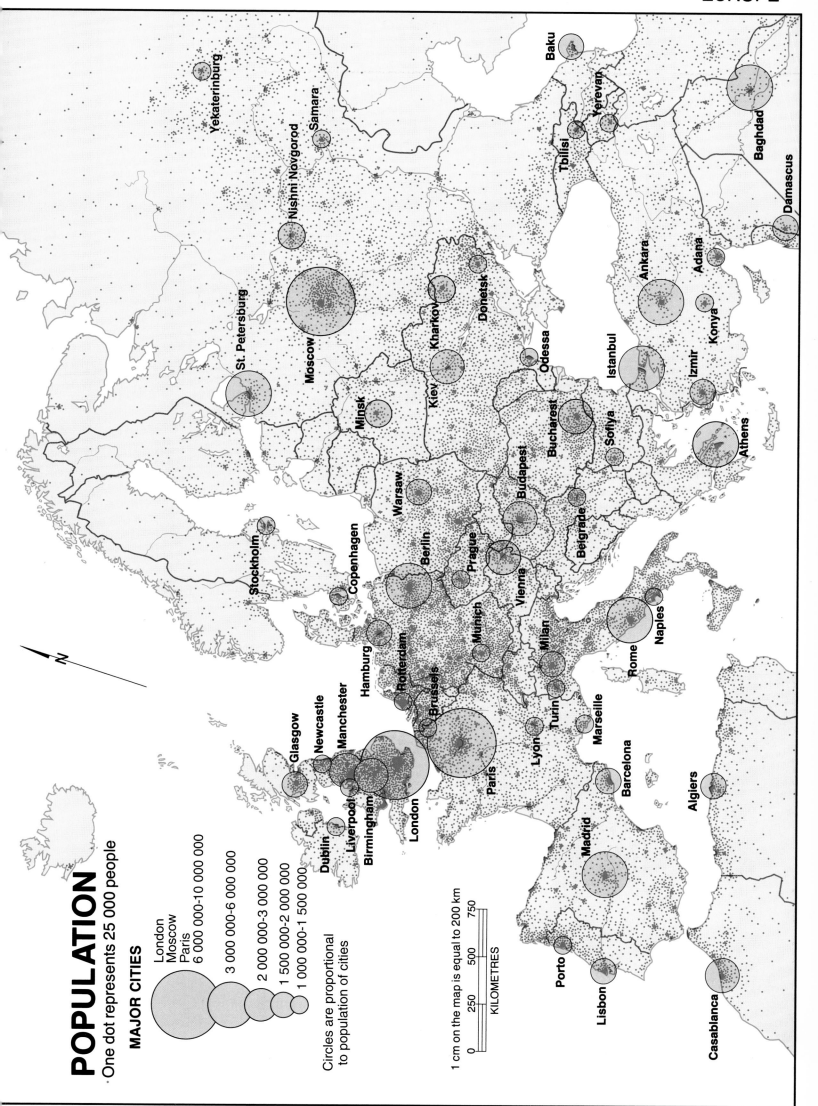

POPULATION

One dot represents 25 000 people

MAJOR CITIES

London
Moscow
Paris
6 000 000-10 000 000

3 000 000-6 000 000

2 000 000-3 000 000

1 500 000-2 000 000

1 000 000-1 500 000

Circles are proportional
to population of cities

1 cm on the map is equal to 200 km

0   250   500   750

KILOMETRES

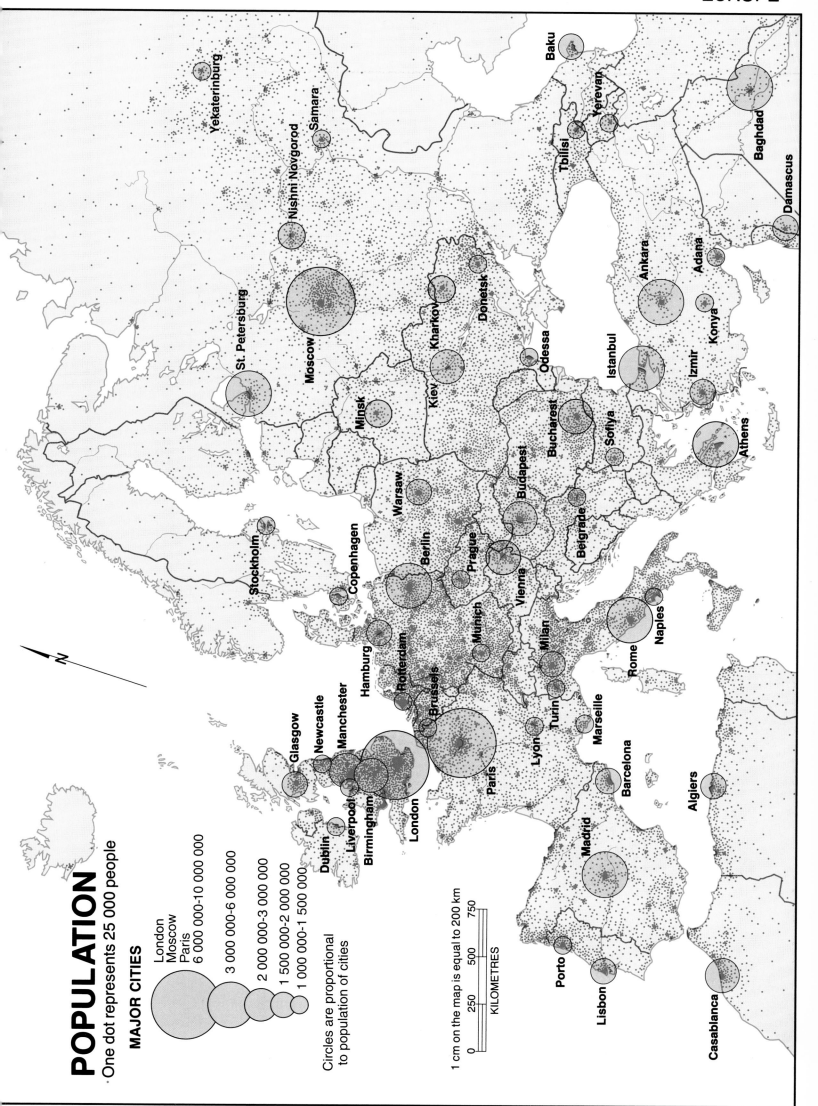

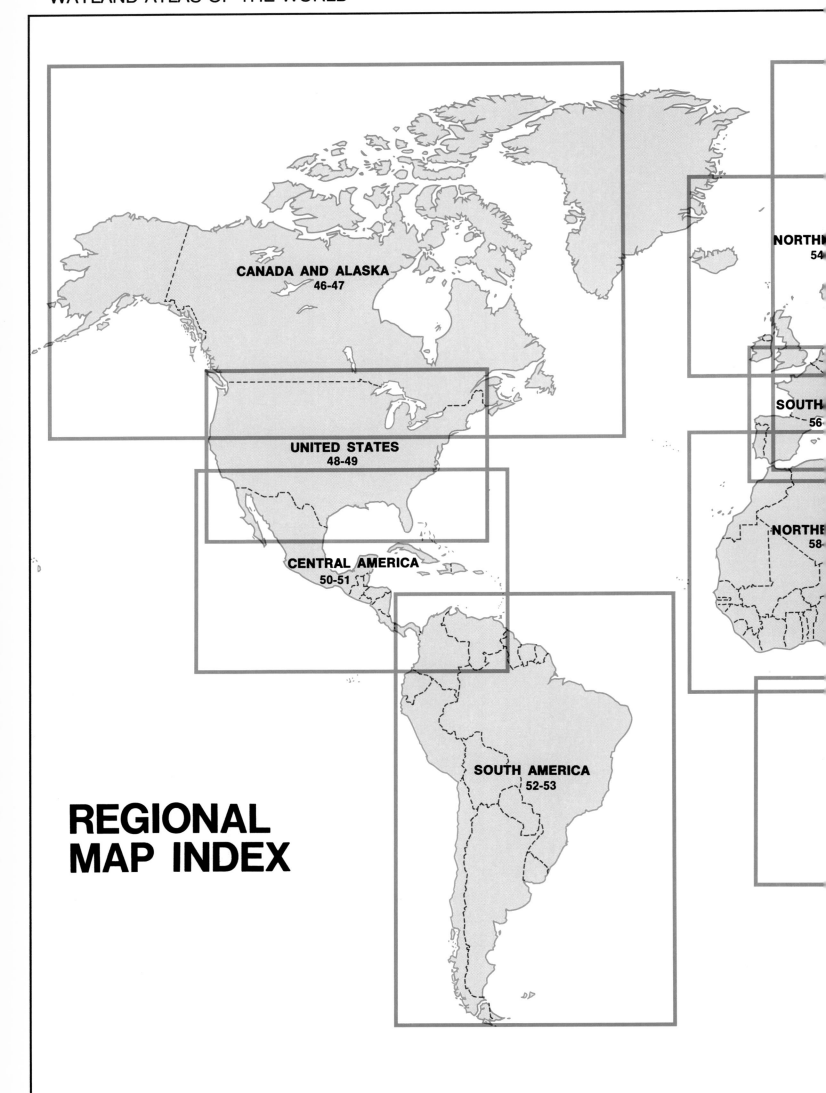

CANADA AND ALASKA
46-47

NORTH
54

UNITED STATES
48-49

SOUTH
56-

CENTRAL AMERICA
50-51

NORTHE
58-

REGIONAL
MAP INDEX

SOUTH AMERICA
52-53

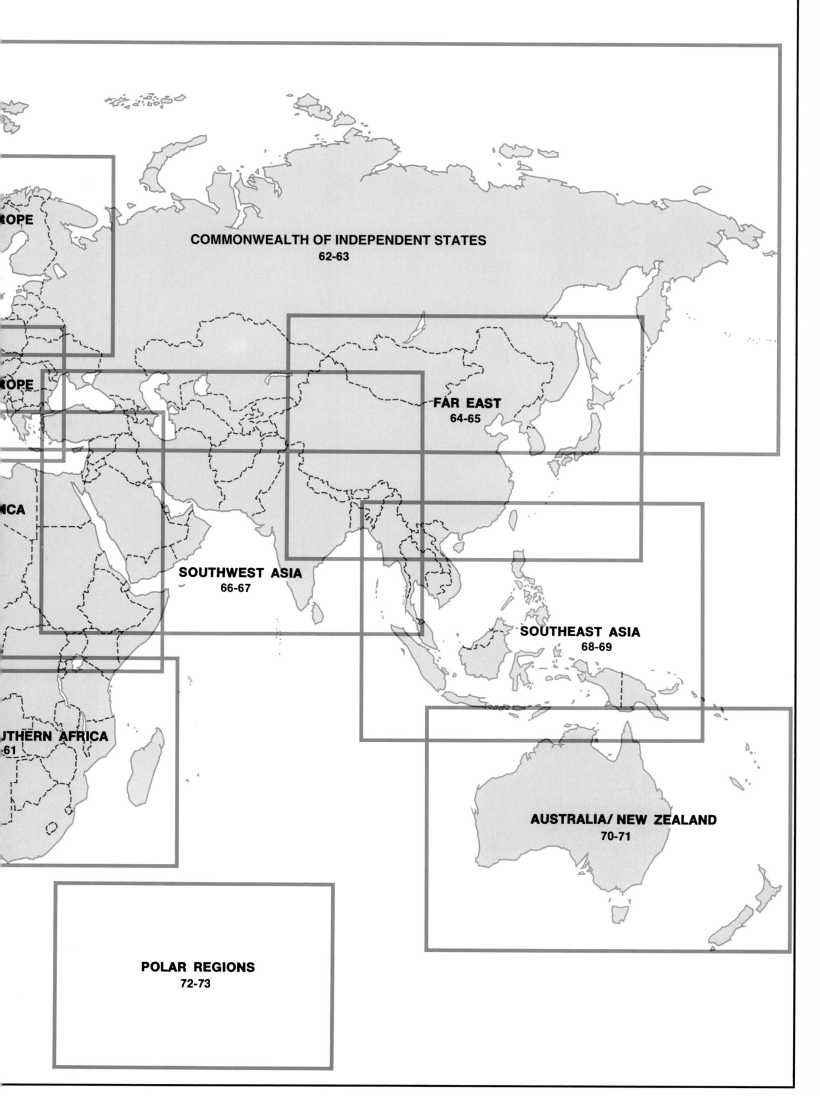

ROPE

ROPE

COMMONWEALTH OF INDEPENDENT STATES
62-63

FAR EAST
64-65

CA

SOUTHWEST ASIA
66-67

SOUTHEAST ASIA
68-69

UTHERN AFRICA
61

AUSTRALIA/ NEW ZEALAND
70-71

POLAR REGIONS
72-73

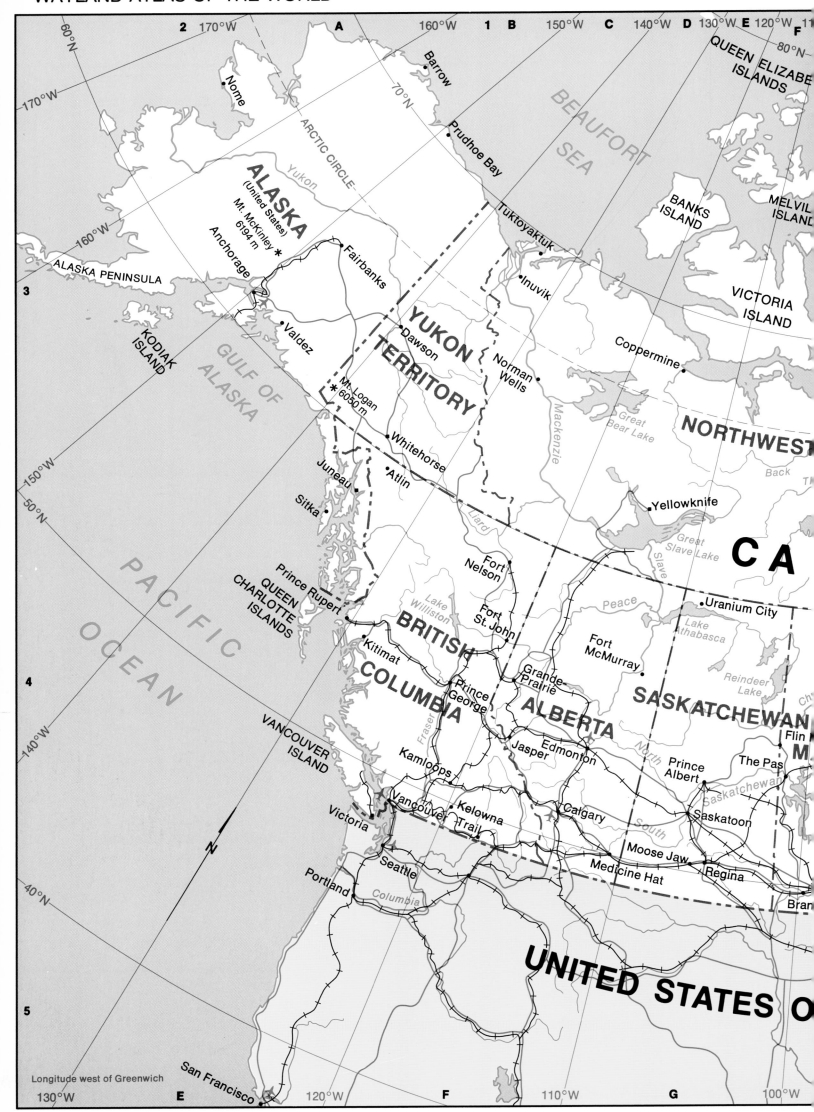

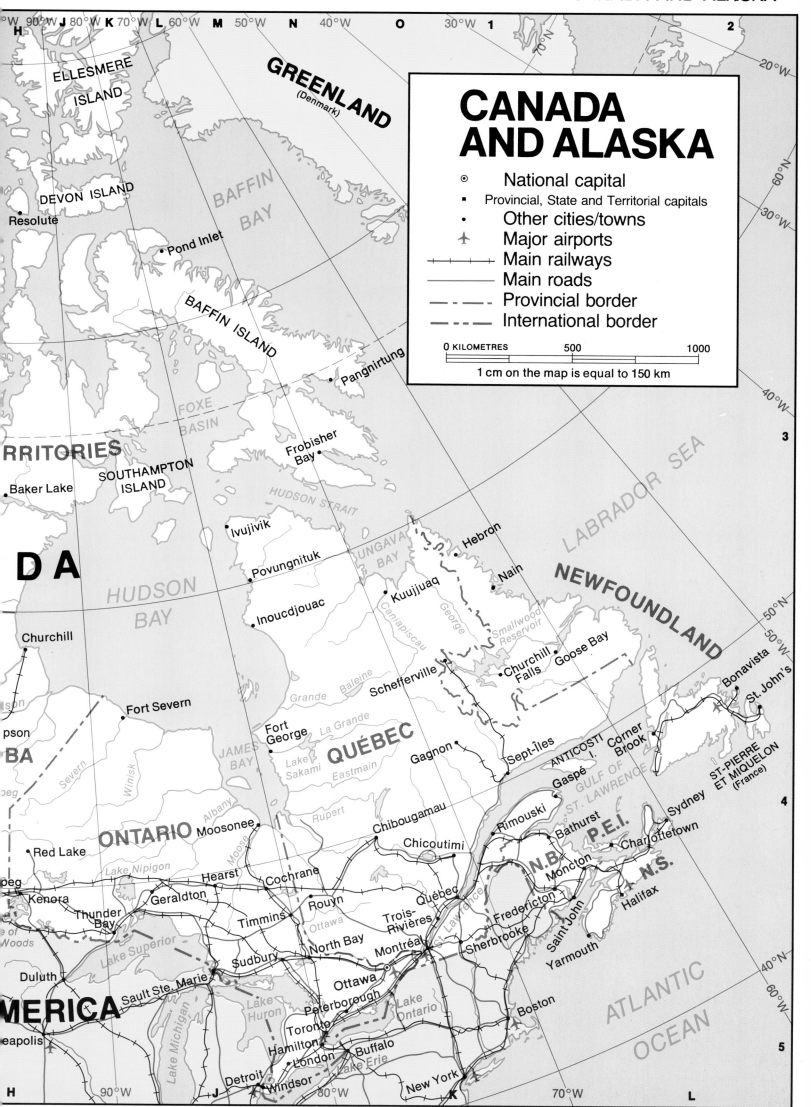

CANADA AND ALASKA

⊙ National capital
▪ Provincial, State and Territorial capitals
• Other cities/towns
✈ Major airports
+—+—+ Main railways
——— Main roads
—·—·— Provincial border
—··—··— International border

0 KILOMETRES 500 1000

1 cm on the map is equal to 150 km

ELLESMERE ISLAND

DEVON ISLAND

Resolute

GREENLAND
(Denmark)

BAFFIN BAY

Pond Inlet

BAFFIN ISLAND

Pangnirtung

FOXE BASIN

RRITORIES

SOUTHAMPTON ISLAND

Baker Lake

Frobisher Bay

HUDSON STRAIT

LABRADOR SEA

D A

Ivujivik

UNGAVA BAY

Hebron

HUDSON BAY

Povungnituk

Nain

NEWFOUNDLAND

Inoucdjouac

Kuujjuaq

Caniapiscau

George

Smallwood Reservoir

Churchill

Churchill Falls

Goose Bay

Bonavista

St. John's

Fort Severn

Scheffervile

Grande Baleine

Sept-Îles

ANTICOSTI I.

Corner Brook

ST-PIERRE ET MIQUELON (France)

pson

Fort George

La Grande

QUÉBEC

Gagnon

Gaspé

GULF OF ST. LAWRENCE

Sydney

BA

Severn

JAMES BAY

Lake Sakami

Eastmain

Rupert

Rimouski

Bathurst

P.E.I.

Charlottetown

Winisk

Albany

Moosonee

Chibougamau

Chicoutimi

N.B.

Moncton

N.S.

Red Lake

ONTARIO

Lake Nipigon

Moose

Hearst

Cochrane

Québec

Fredericton

Halifax

Kenora

Geraldton

Rouyn

Trois-Rivières

Saint John

peg

Thunder Bay

Timmins

Ottawa

North Bay

Montréal

Sherbrooke

Yarmouth

e of Woods

Lake Superior

Sudbury

St. Lawrence

Duluth

Sault Ste. Marie

Lake Huron

Ottawa

Boston

ATLANTIC OCEAN

MERICA

Lake Michigan

Peterborough

Lake Ontario

eapolis

Toronto

Hamilton

London

Buffalo

Detroit

Windsor

Lake Erie

New York

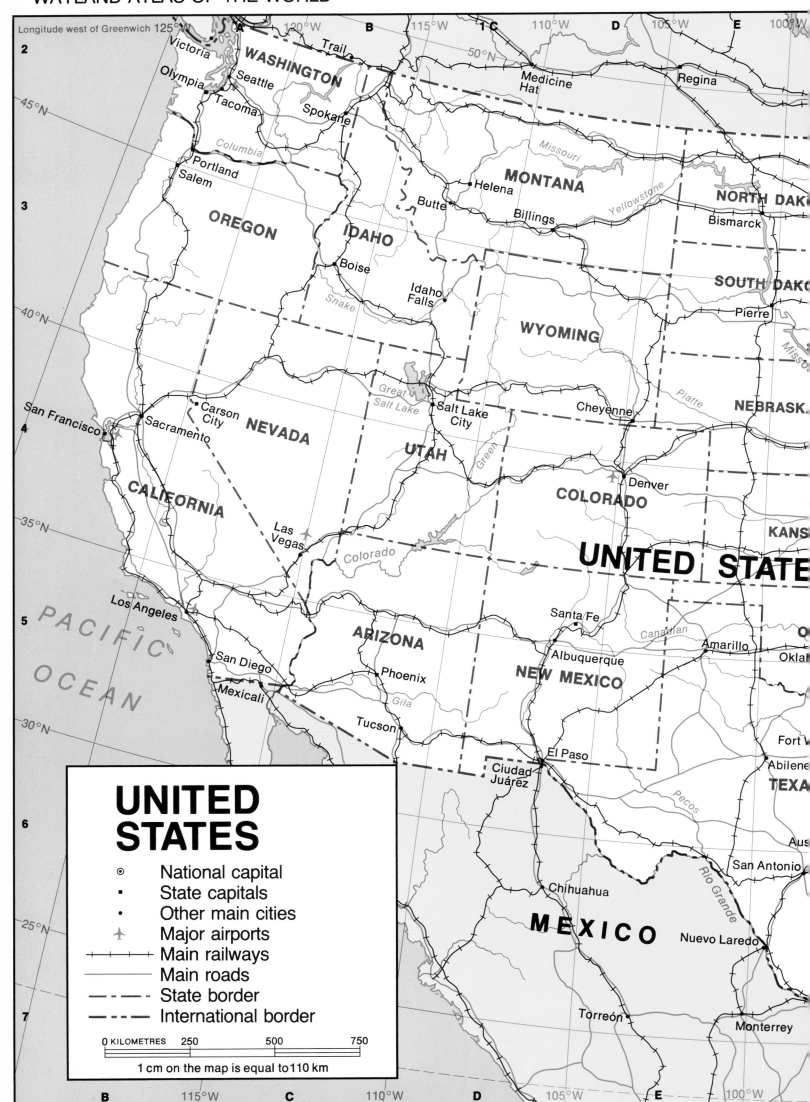

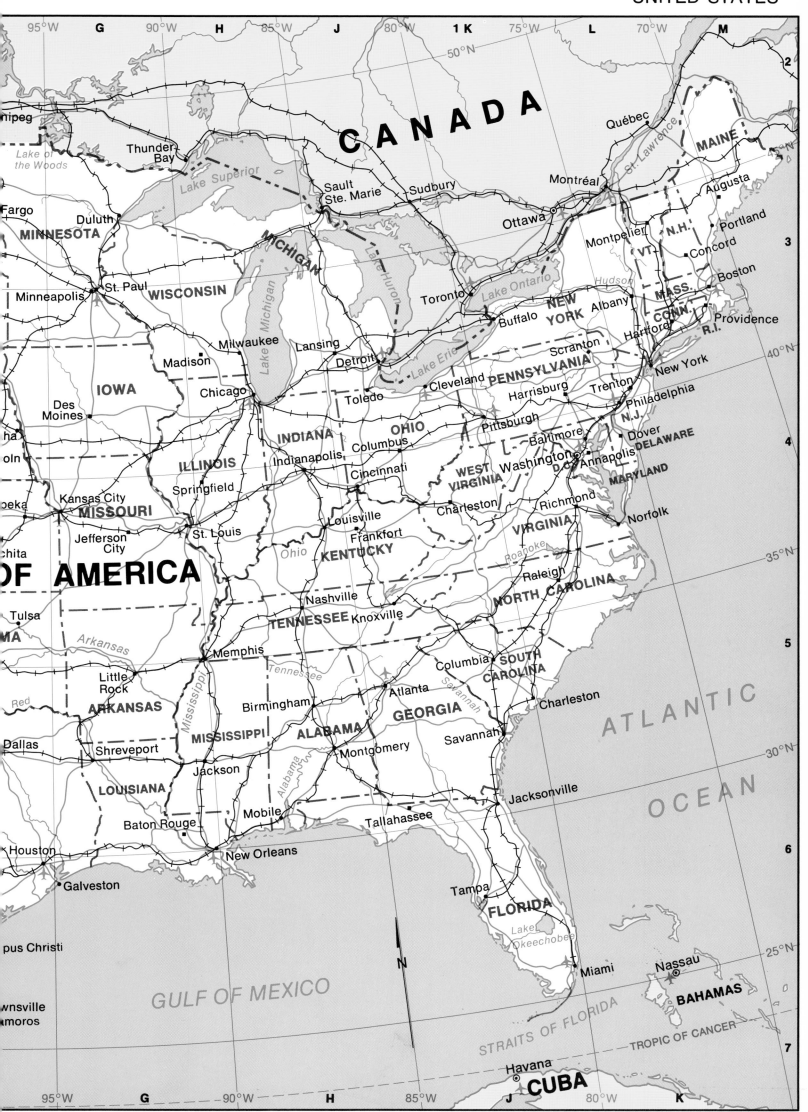

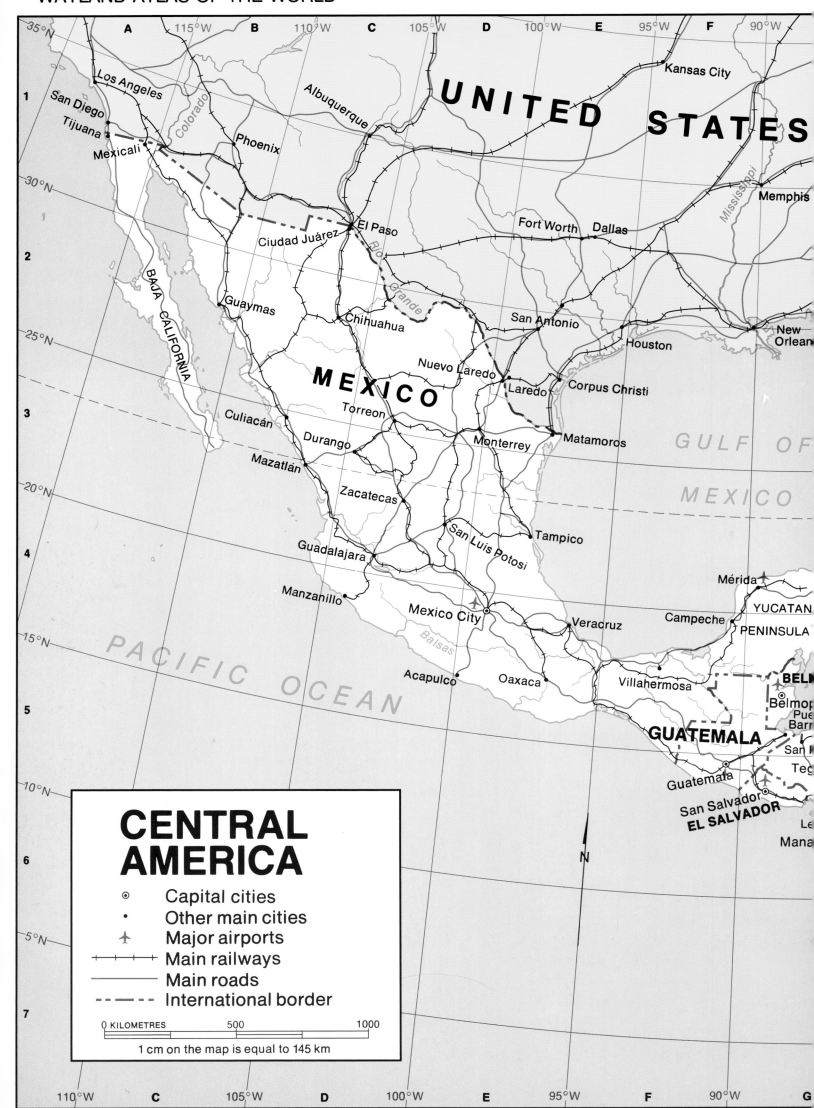

CENTRAL AMERICA

⊙   Capital cities

•   Other main cities

✈   Major airports

╁╁╁   Main railways

   Main roads

– ∙ – ∙ –   International border

0 KILOMETRES   500   1000

1 cm on the map is equal to 145 km

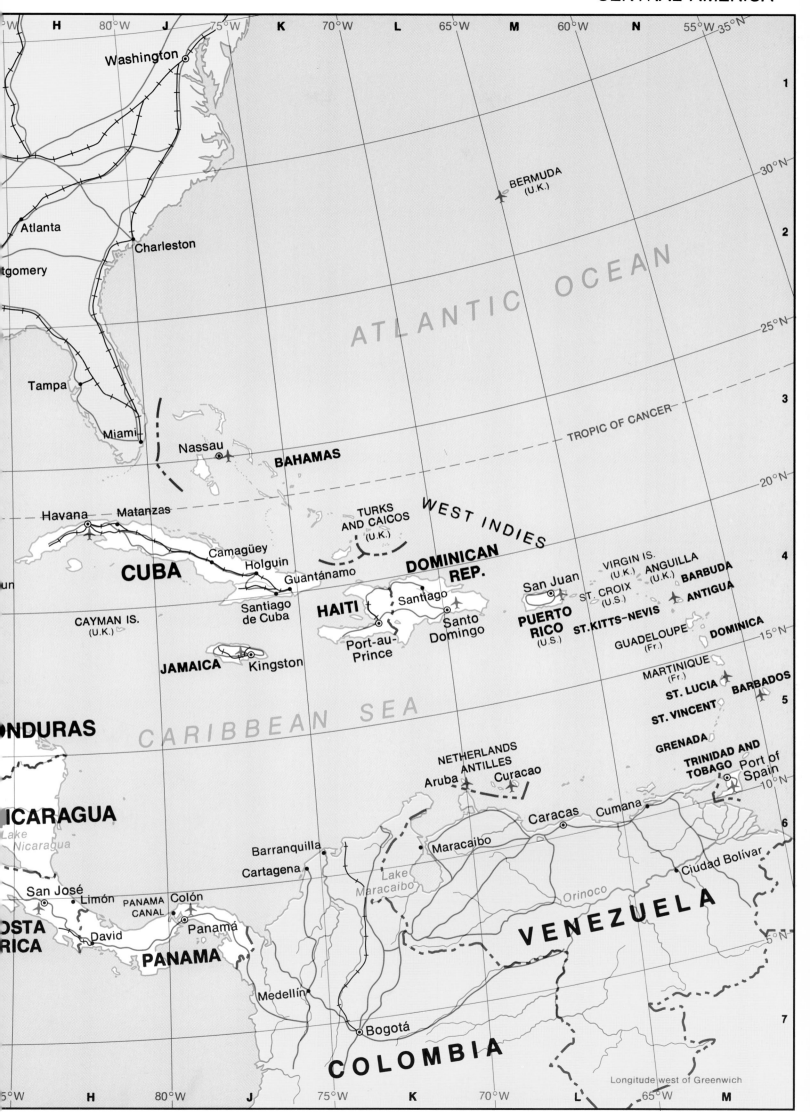

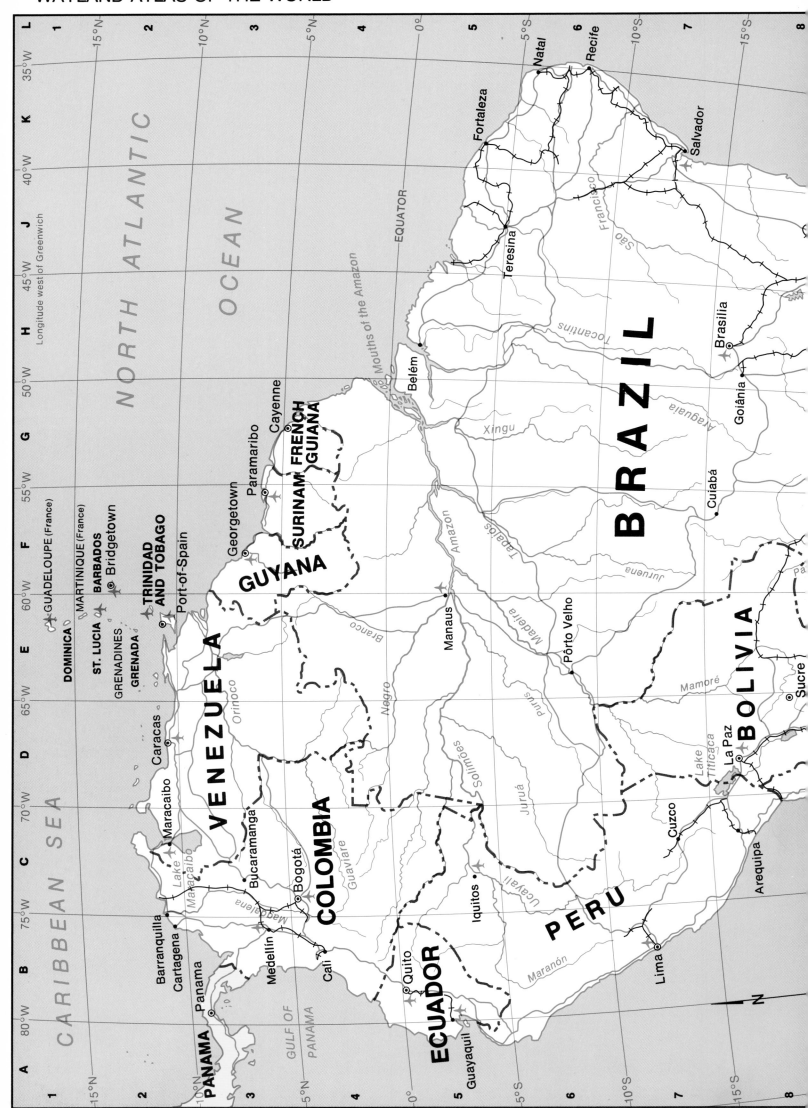

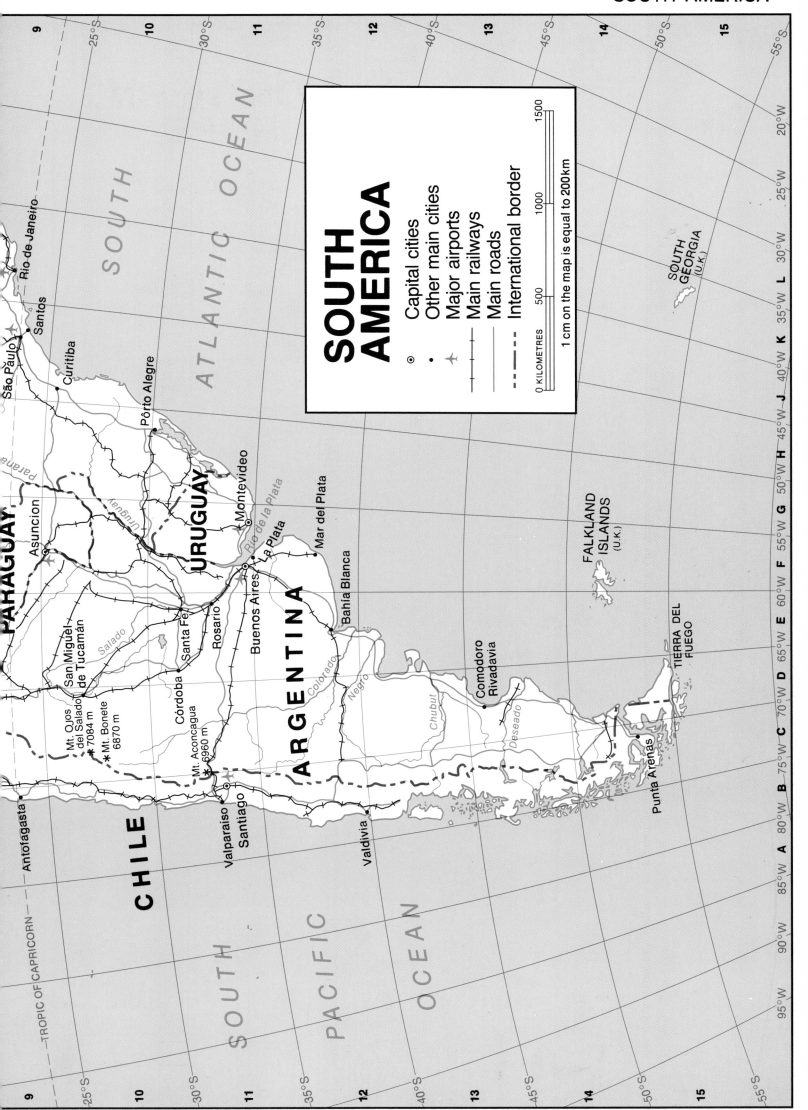

SOUTH AMERICA

- ⊙ Capital cities
- • Other main cities
- ✈ Major airports
- Main railways
- Main roads
- International border

0 KILOMETRES   500   1000   1500

1 cm on the map is equal to 200km

SOUTH ATLANTIC OCEAN

SOUTH PACIFIC OCEAN

PARAGUAY

URUGUAY

ARGENTINA

CHILE

Rio de Janeiro

Santos

São Paulo

Curitiba

Pôrto Alegre

Montevideo

Mar del Plata

Asuncion

San Miguel de Tucamán

Mt. Ojos del Salado 7084 m

Mt. Bonete 6870 m

Córdoba

Santa Fe

Rosario

Mt. Aconcagua 6960 m

Buenos Aires

La Plata

Rio de la Plata

Bahía Blanca

Comodoro Rivadavia

Antofagasta

Valparaíso

Santiago

Valdivia

Punta Arenas

TIERRA DEL FUEGO

FALKLAND ISLANDS (U.K.)

SOUTH GEORGIA (U.K.)

TROPIC OF CAPRICORN

Paraná

Uruguay

Salado

Colorado

Negro

Chubut

Deseado

25°S 30°S 35°S 40°S 45°S 50°S 55°S

95°W 90°W 85°W 80°W 75°W 70°W 65°W 60°W 55°W 50°W 45°W 40°W 35°W 30°W 25°W 20°W

A B C D E F G H J K L

9 10 11 12 13 14 15

NORTHERN EUROPE

⊙	National capitals
•	Other main cities
✈	Major airports
┼┼┼┼	Main railways
———	Main roads
– · – · –	International border

0 KILOMETRES   500

1 cm on the map is equal to 80 km

Vatneyri
Olafsvik
Reykjavik
Akureyri
ICELAND
Höfn
ARCTIC CIRCLE

ATLANTIC
OCEAN

FAEROE
ISLANDS
(Denmark)

NORWEGIAN
SEA

Trondh
Dombas
NORWAY
Bergen
Dramm
Stavanger
Kristians

SHETLAND
ISLANDS
(U.K.)

HEBRIDES

ORKNEY
ISLANDS

Inverness
SCOTLAND
Aberdeen
Dundee
Glasgow
Edinburgh
UNITED
KINGDOM

NORTH
SEA

SKAGERRAK
Alborg
DENMARK

Londonderry
NORTHERN
IRELAND
Belfast
Newcastle

Esbjerg
Oden

REPUBLIC
OF IRELAND
Galway
Dublin
Liverpool
Manchester
York
IRISH SEA

Bremerhaven
Hamb

Waterford
Sheffield
ENGLAND

Cork
Birmingham
WALES
Cardiff
Oxford
Norwich
Cambridge
NETHERLANDS
Amsterdam

Bremen
Hannover

Plymouth
Bristol
London
Brighton
Southampton
Rotterdam
Essen
GER
Antwerp
BELGIUM
Dortmund

Prime meridian

Longitude west of Greenwich

ATLANTIC OCEAN

REPUBLIC OF IRELAND

Waterford

Cork

UNITED KINGDOM

Birmingham

Cardiff

Bristol

Plymouth

London

NETHERLANDS

Amsterdam

Rotterdam

Antwerp

Calais

Lille

Brussels

BELGIUM

Liège

LUXEMBOURG

GER

Essen

Bonn

Bremen

Hann

Fra

ENGLISH CHANNEL

CHANNEL ISLANDS (U.K.)

LeHavre

Rouen

Caen

Seine

Paris

Brest

BAY OF BISCAY

Nantes

Tours

Loire

FRANCE

Dijon

Meuse

Rhine

Stu

Zürich

Bern

SWITZERL

Limoges

Lyon

Geneva

Mont Blanc 4807 m

Mila

Bordeaux

Garonne

Rhône

Nîmes

Torino

Ge

Toulouse

Nice

MONACO

La Coruña

Vigo

Oviedo

Bilbao

Burgos

Pamplona

ANDORRA

Zaragoza

Marseille

CORSICA (France)

Bast

Porto

PORTUGAL

Douro

Salamanca

Ebro

SPAIN

Barcelona

SARDINIA (Italy)

Sassari

Lisbon

Madrid

Tagus

Valencia

BALEARIC ISLANDS (Spain)

Palma

Córdoba

Sevilla

Murcia

Alicante

Cagliari

Granada

Cádiz

Mt. Mulhacen 3478 m

Cartagena

Tanger

Málaga

Gibraltar (U.K.)

ALBORAN SEA

Prime meridian

Rabat

MOROCCO

ALGERIA

Longitude west of Greenwich

10°W   5°W   0°   5°E

50°N

45°N

40°N

35°N

A   1   B   2   C   D

A   5°W   B   0°   C   5°E   D

SOUTHERN EUROPE

⊙ Capital city
• Other main cities
✈ Major airports
╫ Main railways
— Main roads
- - - International border

0   KILOMETRES   500

1 cm on the map is equal to 80 km

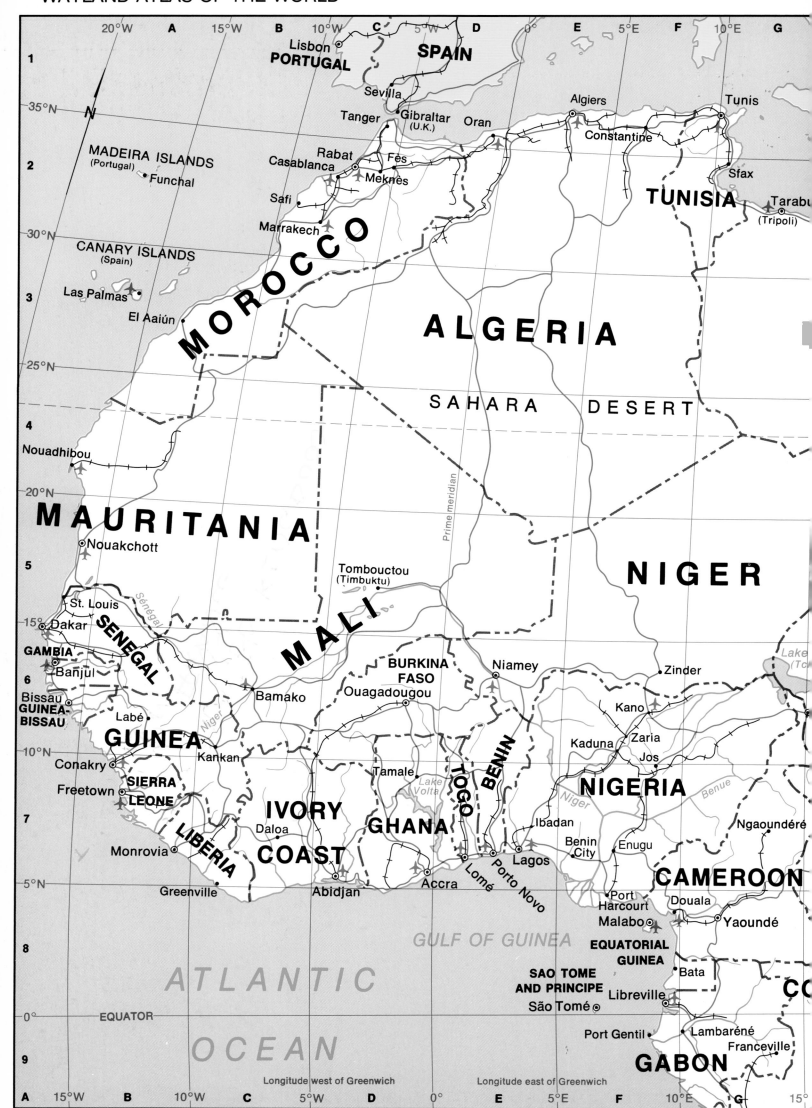

NORTHERN AFRICA

⊙ Capital cities
·   Other main cities
✈ Major airports
┼┼┼┼ Main railways
─── Main roads
─·─·─ International border

0 KILOMETRES   500   1000

1 cm on the map is equal to 172 km

MEDITERRANEAN SEA

nghazi
Tubruq
El Iskandarîya (Alexandria)
Bûr Sa'îd (Port Said)

LIBYAN DESERT

EGYPT

El Qâhira (Cairo)
El Suweis (Suez)

YA

Nile

25°N

Lake Nasser
Aswân
Medina
Riyadh
35°N
30°N

TROPIC OF CANCER

Wadi Halfa

SAUDI ARABIA

Jiddah
Mecca
20°N

HAD

Port Sudan

RED SEA

Atbara

Atbara
Sana'a
REPUBLIC OF YEMEN
15°N

Khartoum
Kassala

El Bahr el Azraq (Blue Nile)

Asmara ERITREA

* Mt. Ras Dashen 4620 m

Aden

GULF OF ADEN

SUDAN

Bahr el Jebel

El Bahr el Azraq (White Nile)

T'ana Hayk

DJIBOUTI
Djibouti
Berbera
10°N

Bahr el 'Arab

Addis Ababa

CENTRAL RICAN REPUBLIC

ETHIOPIA

SOMALIA

Bangassou
Obo
Juba
5°N

Bangui
Oubangui

Lake Turkana (L. Rudolf)

Juba

Zaire (Congo)

Lake Mobutu Sese Seko
UGANDA

KENYA

Muqdisho (Mogadishu)
8

Kisangani
Mt. Ruwenzori 5109 m *
Kampala

Nakuru

Chisimaio (Kismayu)

INDIAN

0°

ZAIRE

Lake Victoria

RWANDA ⊙ Kigali

Nairobi

OCEAN

BURUNDI
Bujumbura
TANZANIA

Mwanza

Mt. Kilimanjaro 5895 m
* M

9

GABON

CONGO

Port Gentil
Lambaréné
Moanda
Franceville
Dolisie
Brazzaville
Pointe Noire
(Angola) CABINDA
Cabinda
Matadi
Kinshasa
Kikwit

REPUB

Lac
Mai-Ndombe
Congo
Kasai
Port
Lusambo
ZA
Kananga
Kam
Kwango

Luanda
Malange

ATLANTIC

OCEAN

Prime meridian

Lobito
Kuito
Luena

ANGOLA

Moçâmedes

Cuneme

Okavango

Kwando

Tsumeb

NAMIBIA

BOTS

KALAHARI

DESERT Gabo

Nossob

Walvis Bay
(South Africa)
Windhoek
Gobabis

TROPIC OF CAPRICORN

Keetmanshoop
Lüderitz

Molopo

REPUE

Kimberley
Bloen

Orange

OF

SOUTH AF

SOUTHERN AFRICA

⊙ Capital cities
• Other main cities
✈ Major airports
┼┼┼┼ Main railways
──── Main roads
─ ─ ─ International border

0 KILOMETRES   500   1000

1 cm on the map is equal to 133km

1
2
3
4
5
6
7

0°
5°E
10°E
15°E
20°E

0°
5°E   A   10°E   B   15°E   C   20°E   D   25

5°S
10°S
15°S
20°S
25°S
30°S

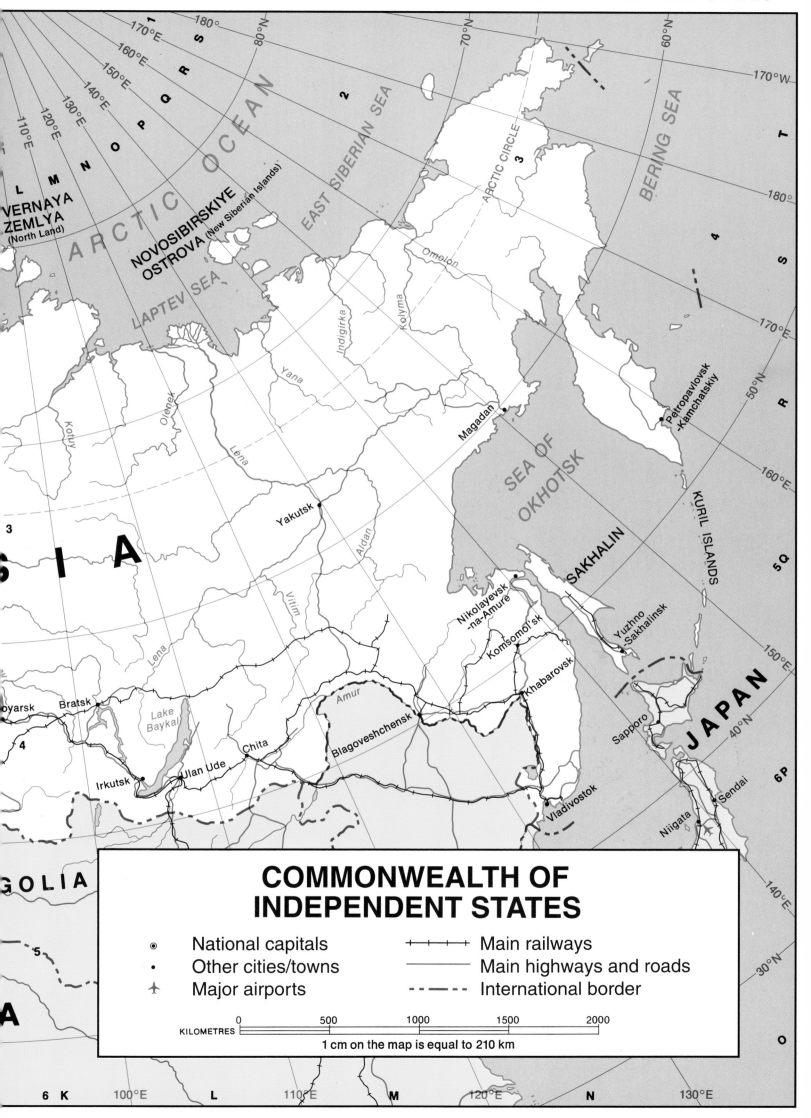

SEVERNAYA ZEMLYA (North Land)

ARCTIC OCEAN

NOVOSIBIRSKIYE OSTROVA (New Siberian Islands)

EAST SIBERIAN SEA

LAPTEV SEA

BERING SEA

ARCTIC CIRCLE

Omolon

Kotuy

Olenek

Indigirka

Yana

Kolyma

Lena

Magadan

Petropavlovsk -Kamchatskiy

SEA OF OKHOTSK

S I A

Yakutsk

Aldan

Vitim

SAKHALIN

KURIL ISLANDS

Nikolayevsk -na-Amure

Komsomol'sk

Yuzhno Sakhalinsk

Lena

Khabarovsk

oyarsk

Bratsk

Lake Baykal

Amur

Blagoveshchensk

JAPAN

Chita

Sapporo

Ulan Ude

Vladivostok

Irkutsk

Niigata

Sendai

GOLIA

COMMONWEALTH OF INDEPENDENT STATES

◎	National capitals	┼┼┼┼┼	Main railways
•	Other cities/towns	───────	Main highways and roads
✈	Major airports	─ ─ ─ ─	International border

KILOMETRES
0   500   1000   1500   2000

1 cm on the map is equal to 210 km

A

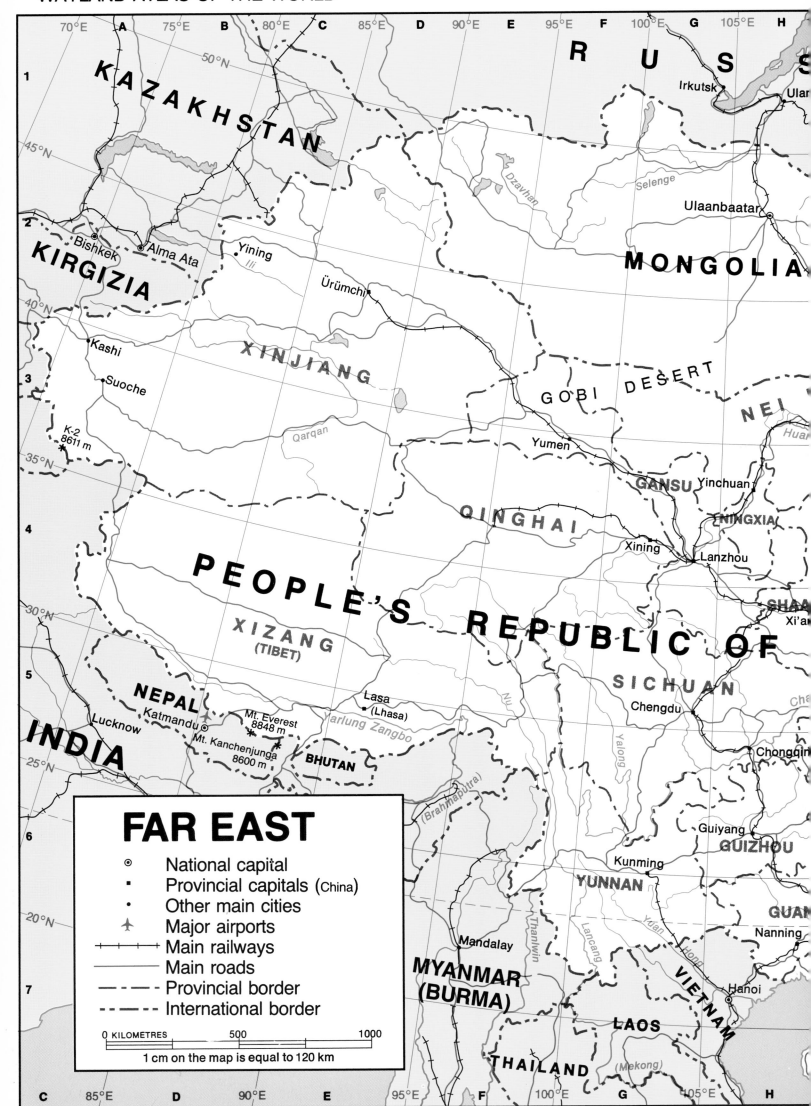

FAR EAST

⊙ National capital
▪ Provincial capitals (China)
· Other main cities
✈ Major airports
+++ Main railways
—— Main roads
—·—·— Provincial border
----- International border

0 KILOMETRES   500   1000

1 cm on the map is equal to 120 km

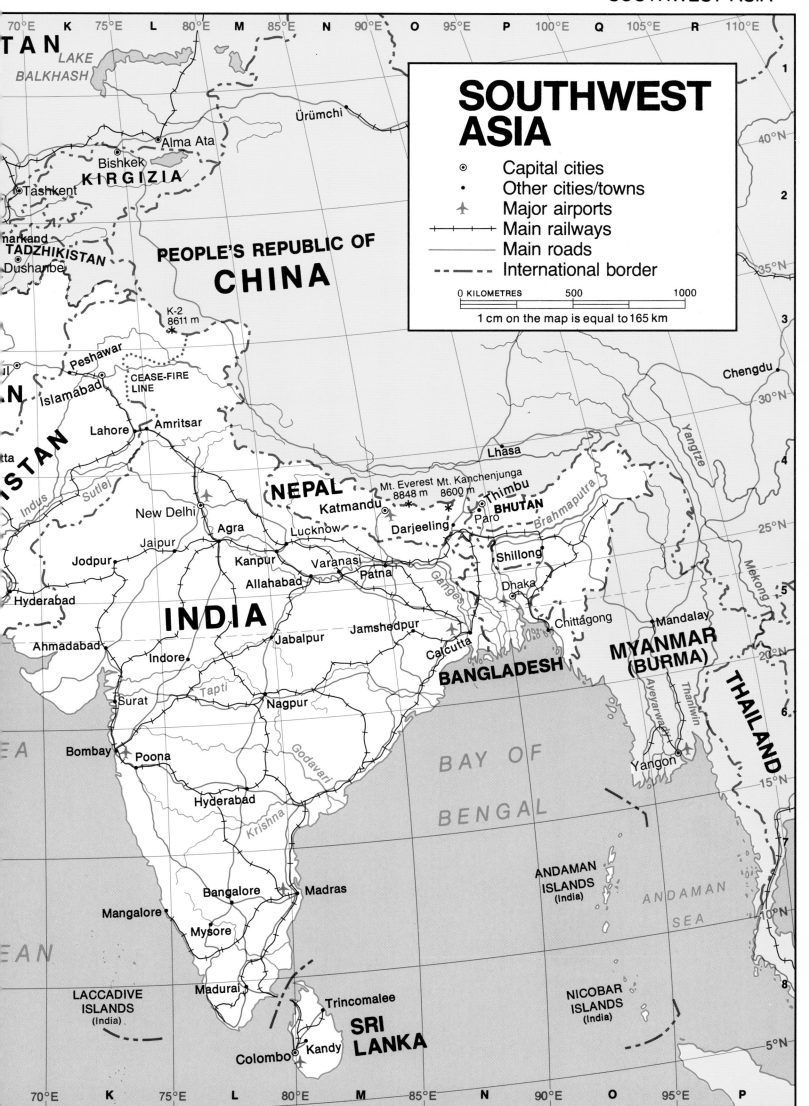

SOUTHWEST ASIA

⊙	Capital cities
•	Other cities/towns
✈	Major airports
┼┼┼┼	Main railways
——	Main roads
– – –	International border

0 KILOMETRES   500   1000

1 cm on the map is equal to 165 km

LAKE BALKHASH

Ürümchi

Alma Ata

Bishkek

KIRGIZIA

Tashkent

amarkand

TADZHIKISTAN

Dushanbe

PEOPLE'S REPUBLIC OF CHINA

K-2 8611 m

Chengdu

Peshawar

CEASE-FIRE LINE

Islamabad

Lahore

Amritsar

Lhasa

NEPAL

Mt. Everest 8848 m

Mt. Kanchenjunga 8600 m

Thimbu

BHUTAN

New Delhi

Katmandu

Paro

Agra

Lucknow

Darjeeling

Shillong

Jaipur

Kanpur

Varanasi

Jodpur

Allahabad

Patna

Indus

Sutlej

Dhaka

Hyderabad

INDIA

Jabalpur

Jamshedpur

Ganges

Brahmaputra

Yangtze

Chittagong

Mandalay

Ahmadabad

Indore

Calcutta

BANGLADESH

MYANMAR (BURMA)

Surat

Tapti

Nagpur

THAILAND

Bombay

Poona

Godavari

BAY OF

Mekong

Ayeyarwady

Thanlwin

Hyderabad

Krishna

BENGAL

Yangon

Bangalore

Madras

ANDAMAN ISLANDS (India)

Mangalore

ANDAMAN SEA

Mysore

LACCADIVE ISLANDS (India)

Madurai

Trincomalee

NICOBAR ISLANDS (India)

SRI LANKA

Colombo   Kandy

70°E   K   75°E   L   80°E   M   85°E   N   90°E   O   95°E   P   100°E   Q   105°E   R   110°E

INDIA

Myitkyina

Mandalay

MYANMAR
(BURMA)

Sittwe

Kengtung

Yangon

Chiang
Mai

Mawlamyine

THAILAND

Krung Thep
(Bangkok)

Mergui

ANDAMAN
ISLANDS
(India)

ANDAMAN
SEA

NICOBAR
ISLANDS
(India)

PEOPLE'S REPUBLIC OF
CHINA

Kunming

Lao Cai

Guangzhou

HONG KONG
(U.K.)

Zhanjiang

Kaohsiung

TAIWAN

Taipei

LUZON STRAIT

Luang
Prabang

Hanoi

Haiphong

HAINAN

Vientiane

LAOS

Hue

Da-nang

VIETNAM

Ubon
Ratchathani

CAMBODIA

Phnom
Penh

Nha-trang

Ho Chi Minh City
(Saigon)

SOUTH

CHINA

SEA

Aparri

LUZON

Manila

MINDORO

PANAY

Iloilo

NEGROS

PALAWAN

SULU
SEA

Zamboanga

Sandakan

Surat Thani

GULF OF
THAILAND

10°N

Banda Aceh

Pinang

Kota Baharu

MALAYA

Medan

STRAIT OF MALACCA

Kuala
Lumpur

SINGAPORE

Paloh

Kuching

MALAYSIA

BRUNEI
Bandar Seri
Begawan

SARAWAK

SABAH

BORNEO

CELEBES
SEA

SUMATRA

Padang

Pontianak

Kapuas

EQUATOR

Samarinda

MAKASSAR STRAIT

BANGKA

Palembang

Barito

SULAWESI

Banjarmasin

Ujung
Padang

INDIAN OCEAN

Telukbetung

Jakarta

Bandung

JAVA

Yogyakarta

Surabaya

INDONESIA

BALI

Denpasar

Mataram

LOMBOK

SUMBAWA

Raba

Memboro

Baing

FLORES

Ruteng

SUMBA

Larar

Kupang

TIM

10°S

20°N

2

3

0°

4

5

1

A 100°E B 110°E C 120°E

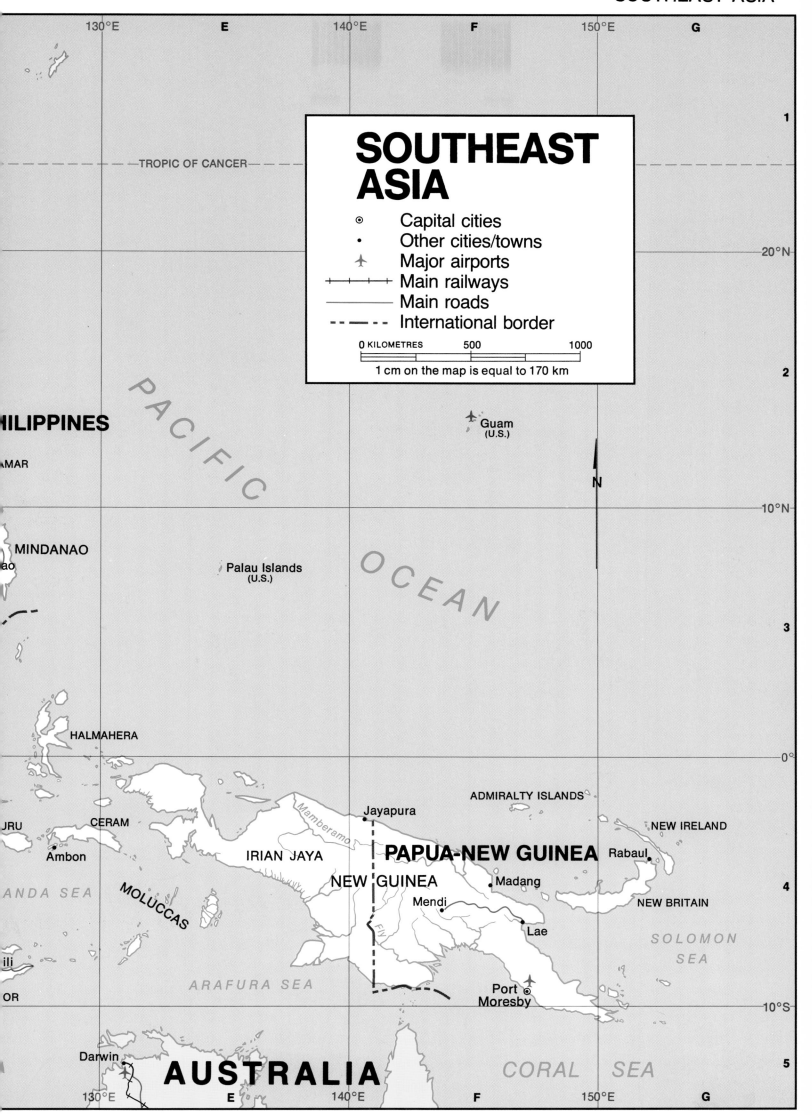

SOUTHEAST ASIA

⊙ Capital cities
· Other cities/towns
✈ Major airports
╁─╁─╁ Main railways
───── Main roads
─ ─ ─ ─ International border

0 KILOMETRES   500   1000

1 cm on the map is equal to 170 km

130°E   E   140°E   F   150°E   G

1

TROPIC OF CANCER

20°N

2

PHILIPPINES

PACIFIC

MAR

✈ Guam
(U.S.)

N

MINDANAO

ao

10°N

Palau Islands
(U.S.)

OCEAN

3

HALMAHERA

0°

ADMIRALTY ISLANDS

Jayapura

NEW IRELAND

JRU   CERAM

Mamberamo

PAPUA-NEW GUINEA   Rabaul

Ambon

IRIAN JAYA

NEW GUINEA

· Madang

4

ANDA SEA

MOLUCCAS

Mendi

NEW BRITAIN

Lae

SOLOMON
SEA

ili

Fly

ARAFURA SEA

Port ⊙
Moresby

10°S

OR

Darwin

CORAL   SEA

5

AUSTRALIA

130°E   E   140°E   F   150°E   G

AUSTRALIA AND NEW ZEALAND

⊙	National capitals	╀╀╀╀	Main railways
▪	State capitals	────	Main roads
•	Other cities/towns	─ · ─ · ─	State borders
✈	Major airports	─ ·· ─ ·· ─	International borders

0 KILOMETRES   500   1000   1500

1 cm on the map is equal to 152 km

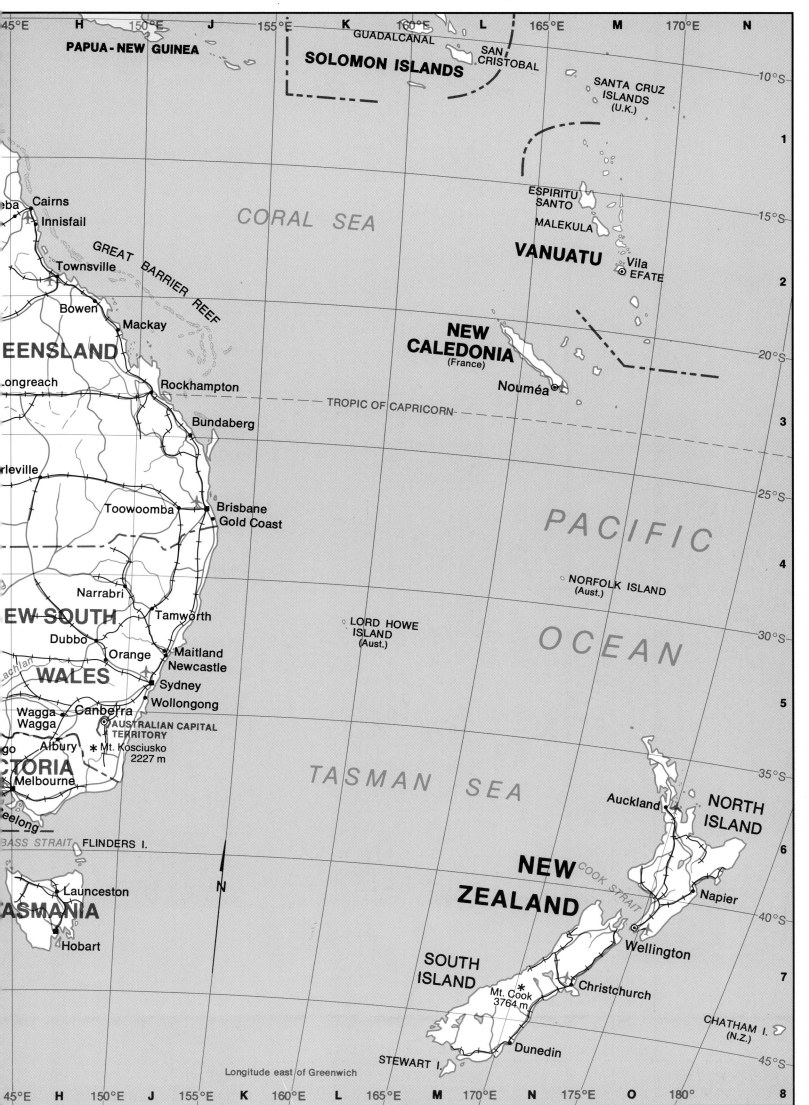

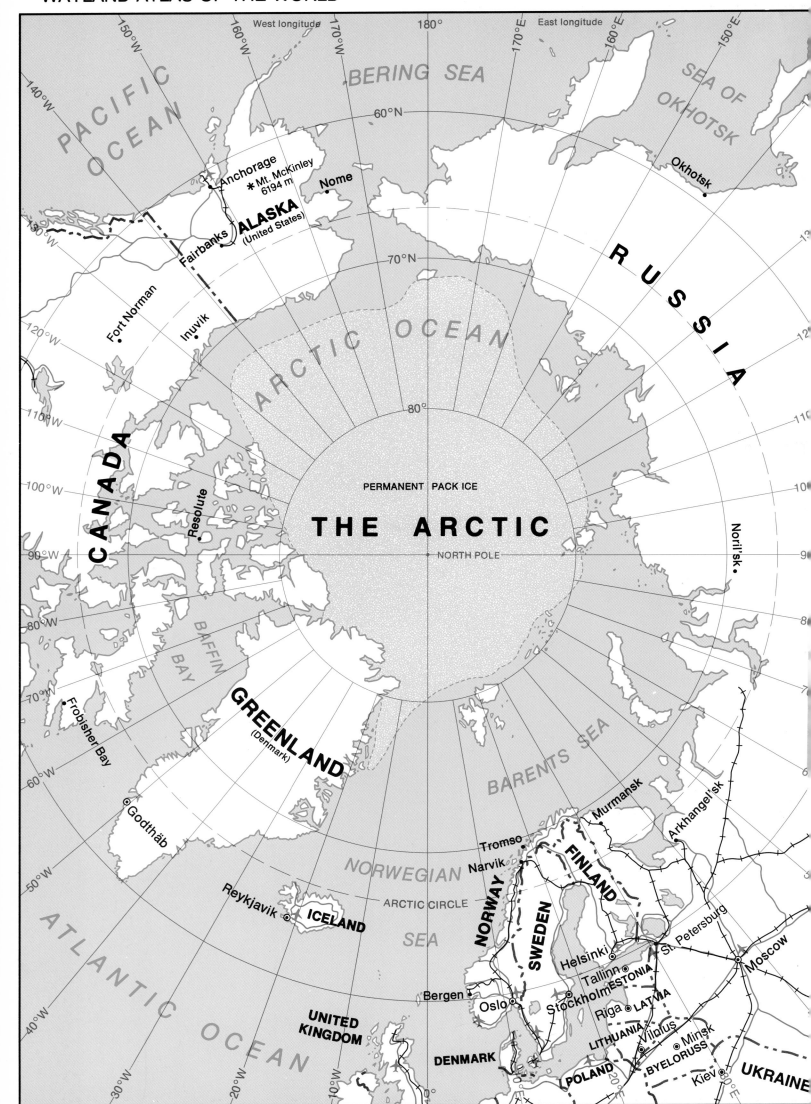

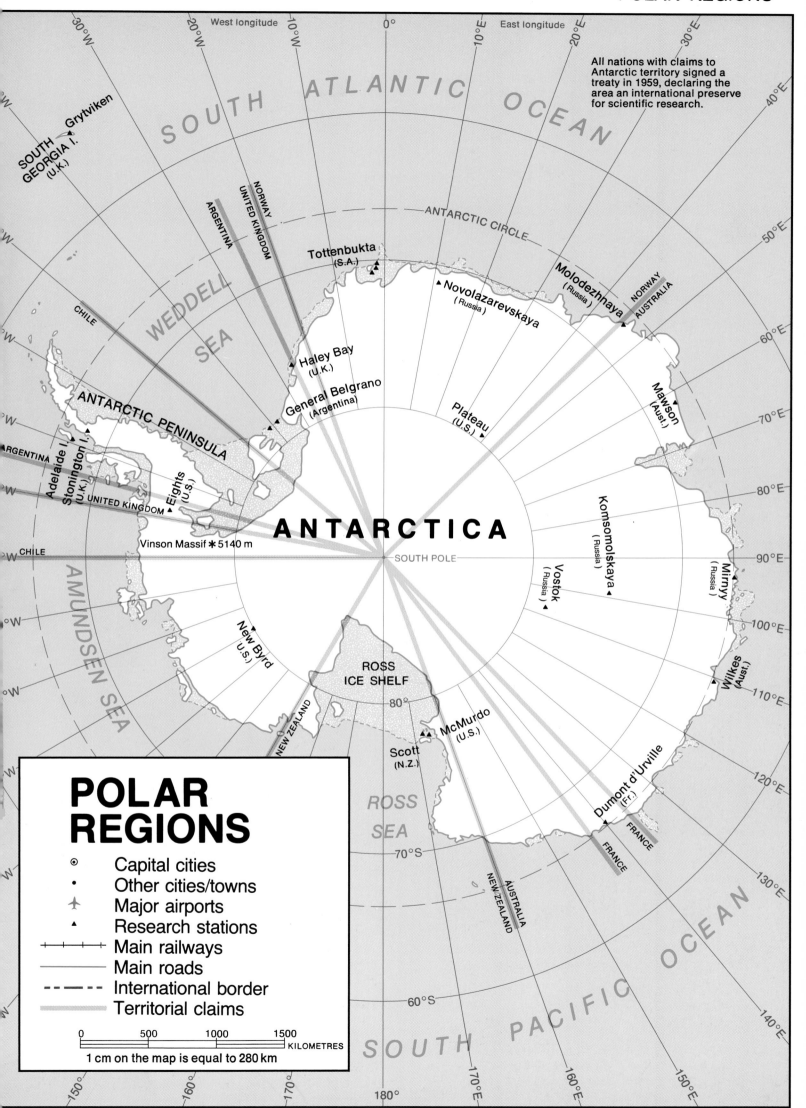

SOUTH ATLANTIC OCEAN

West longitude

East longitude

All nations with claims to Antarctic territory signed a treaty in 1959, declaring the area an international preserve for scientific research.

ANTARCTIC CIRCLE

SOUTH GEORGIA I. (U.K.)
Grytviken

NORWAY
ARGENTINA
UNITED KINGDOM

WEDDELL SEA

Tottenbukta (S.A.)

Novolazarevskaya (Russia)

Molodezhnaya (Russia)

NORWAY
AUSTRALIA

CHILE

Haley Bay (U.K.)

General Belgrano (Argentina)

Plateau (U.S.)

Mawson (Aust.)

ANTARCTIC PENINSULA

ARGENTINA

Adelaide I.
Stonington I. (U.K.)

UNITED KINGDOM

Eights (U.S.)

Komsomolskaya (Russia)

Mirnyy (Russia)

CHILE

Vinson Massif ✳ 5140 m

ANTARCTICA

SOUTH POLE

Vostok (Russia)

AMUNDSEN SEA

New Byrd U.S.)

ROSS ICE SHELF

Wilkes (Aust.)

NEW ZEALAND

McMurdo (U.S.)

Scott (N.Z.)

Dumont d'Urville (Fr.)

FRANCE

ROSS SEA

FRANCE

AUSTRALIA
NEW ZEALAND

SOUTH PACIFIC OCEAN

POLAR REGIONS

⊙ Capital cities
• Other cities/towns
✈ Major airports
▲ Research stations
┼┼┼┼┼ Main railways
───── Main roads
── ── ── International border
━━━━━ Territorial claims

0   500   1000   1500
KILOMETRES

1 cm on the map is equal to 280 km

GLOSSARY

Arab League: an association of twenty-one Arab states and the P.L.O.formed in 1945 to promote economic and military co-operation.

Association of South East Asian Nations: an association of six South East Asian countries, formed in 1967. It aims to speed up the economic and cultural development of its members.

basin: a hollow or trough in the earth's surface. See also drainage basin.

bauxite: a mineral that looks like clay, from which aluminium is produced.

calorie: a metric unit for measuring energy.

climate: the usual kind of weather occurring at one place over a number of years, including conditions of heat and cold, moisture and dryness, cloud and wind.

Commonwealth of Independent States (C.I.S.): a loose association of independent republics formed in December 1991 on the break up of the former Soviet Union.

Commonwealth of Nations: an association of forty-nine independent countries made up of former members of the British Empire.

Communist states: countries in which land, factories, shops, and services are owned by the state.

conifer: a tree that bears cones and is green all year round. It often has needles instead of broad leaves.

continental shelf: the shallower area of ocean floor that borders on the continents.

copper: a reddish-brown metal that conducts heat and electricity well and does not rust easily.

cyclone: a violent storm with rain and high winds, that rotate round a moving area of high pressure, which forms in the tropics. In the Pacific Ocean it is called a typhoon and in the Caribbean Sea it is called a hurricane.

dairy farming: a type of farming where cows are raised for their milk.

desert: a region of very low rainfall. Vegetation is sparse.

drainage basin: the total area drained by a river and its tributaries.

earthquake: movement along a fault in the earth's crust which results in a trembling or shaking of the surface.

elevation: the height of land above sea level, measured in metres.

Equator: the 0° of latitude which circles the earth, midway between the North and South poles.

European Community: an association of European countries whose aim is to achieve full co-operation and economic unity among its members.

glacier: a great field of ice that is formed from snow on high ground. The snow is compressed by its own weight and forms ice, which then moves slowly down a mountain slope or along a valley.

grain farming: a type of farming where grains, such as wheat and oats, are the major crop.

gulf: a large ocean bay, for example, the Gulf of Mexico.

highlands: mountainous regions. Areas of high elevation where the climate varies with the height of the land as well as with latitude.

humid continental zone: a climatic region where the temperature varies widely with warm summers and cold winters.

humid subtropical zone: a climatic region where the temperature is hot in summer and mild in the winter. Rain falls all year round, with a yearly total of at least 100 cm.

hurricane: the name given to tropical cyclones that occur in the late summer and autumn in the West Indies and Caribbean.

hydro-electric: the electric power made by turbines driven by water under high pressure.

intensive farming: a type of farming where high yields of produce are grown on small plots of land, for example, fruit and vegetable farming.

iron ore: common mineral from which a hard, strong metal is made. This is used for tools and machinery and is also necessary for the making of steel.

landform: a natural formation of the earth's surface, for example, a mountain, island, or plain.

latitude: imaginary lines, running east-west around the earth used to locate places and to measure the distance north and south of the Equator. The distance between these lines is measured in degrees (°).

lead: a heavy, grey metal used in combination with other metals.

life expectancy: the average number of years a person, at birth, is expected to live.

literacy: the ability to read and write.

livestock ranching: a type of farming where cattle are raised for their meat.

longitude: imaginary lines running north-south around the earth, used to locate places. Each line passes through the North and South Poles. The distance between these lines is measured in degrees (°). Longitude is measured east and west from the Prime Meridian.

marine middle latitudes: a climatic region with rainfall in all seasons, mild winters, and cool summers.

Mediterranean zone: a climatic region with hot, dry summers and mild, wet winters.

meridian: an imaginary curved line that measures longitude on the earth's surface and passes through the North and South poles. See also longitude.

mixed farming: different types of farming (grain, dairy, vegetable, etc.) on one farm.

molybdenum: a heavy, silvery-white, metallic element used in industry to harden steel.

natural gas: a gas formed naturally in the ground, used as a heating fuel.

nickel: a hard metal that is often used in combination with other metals.

nomadic herding: a type of agriculture where the inhabitants of a region move from place to place throughout the year in search of pasture for their grazing animals.

nuclear energy: the power gained from splitting the atom of a material such as uranium.

oil: see petroleum.

Organization of American States (O.A.S.): an association of thirty-one countries in North and South American founded in 1948 for co-operation on economic matters.

Pampas: the grassy plains surrounding the estuary of the Plate River in South America.

peninsula: a piece of land surrounded on three sides by water, for example, Nova Scotia.

permafrost: ground that is permanently frozen because of the cold climate. Permafrost varies in depth from a few centimetres to many metres.

petroleum (oil): a liquid found in the earth that is flammable and is used to make petrol.

plain: a large area of fairly level land, for example, the Great Plains in North America.

plantation agriculture: a type of agriculture where one or two crops only are grown for commercial purposes, for example, tea, bananas, and sugar cane.

plateau: a large area of fairly level land that is raised above the surrounding area, for example, the Laurentian Plateau.

precipitation: moisture that falls to the earth. Rain, snow, and hail are types of precipitation.

rice farming: a type of farming where rice is grown as the major crop.

scale: the size of an area or distance as shown on a map representing the actual size. For example, one centimetre on a map may represent an actual distance of 130 kilometres on earth.

semi-desert: a climatic region with enough rainfall to support some types of vegetation.

statistics: a collection of facts and figures about, people, places and things.

steel: a combination of iron and carbon hardened by heat into a very strong, hard metal.

steppe: a region of short grass prairie occurring in eastern Europe, South America, and Africa.

strait: a narrow passage of water connecting two larger bodies of water, for example, Strait of Malacca between Malaya and Sumatra.

sub-arctic zone: the region south of the tundra, where the climate is made up of long, extremely cold winters and short, cool summers.

subsistence farming: a type of agriculture where the farmers produce only enough for their own needs and do not have any surplus crops to sell at the market.

subtropical humid zone: climatic region with warm, wet summers and cool, drier winters.

tar sands: deposits of sand where each grain is coated by a film of oil.

temperate hardwood: a tree with dense wood and with broad leaves, rather than needles. These trees lose their leaves during cold weather.

time zone: an area on the earth's surface in which all places have the same time. The International Date Line marks the beginning and the end of the 24 time zones throughout the world.

tin: a silver-coloured metal that is soft and easily shaped.

tornado: an extremely violent funnel-shaped storm that covers a small area of ground.

tropical hardwood: a tree with dense wood and broad leaves which grows in hot climates.

tropical zone: climatic region where the weather is hot all year round, with high amounts of rainfall.

Tropic of Cancer: the parallel of latitude 23°30'N, which is the extreme northern position at which the sun appears to be directly overhead at noon.

Tropic of Capricorn: the parallel of latitude 23°30'S, which is the extreme southern position at which the sun appears to be directly overhead at noon.

tundra: the treeless plains of northern North America and northern Europe and Asia in the latitude of the Arctic Circle, which have a climate of long, severe winters and short, cool summers.

typhoon: a tropical cyclone of high winds and very heavy rainfall which occurs most often in the China Sea during late summer and early autumn.

uranium: a radio-active metal used in nuclear reactions.

volcano: an opening in the earth's crust through which molten rock from deep in the earth forces its way to the surface under pressure.

zinc: a bluish-white metal used in roofs, electric batteries, paint, and medicine.

WORLD STATISTICS

THE EARTH: PHYSICAL FEATURES

The Earth: Basic Facts

	km²	% of total area
Area of the earth's surface	510 000 000	100.0
Area of land surface	150 000 000	29.4
Area of water surface	360 000 000	70.6

Volume	1 083 230 × 10⁶ km³

Mass	5.9 × 10²¹ t

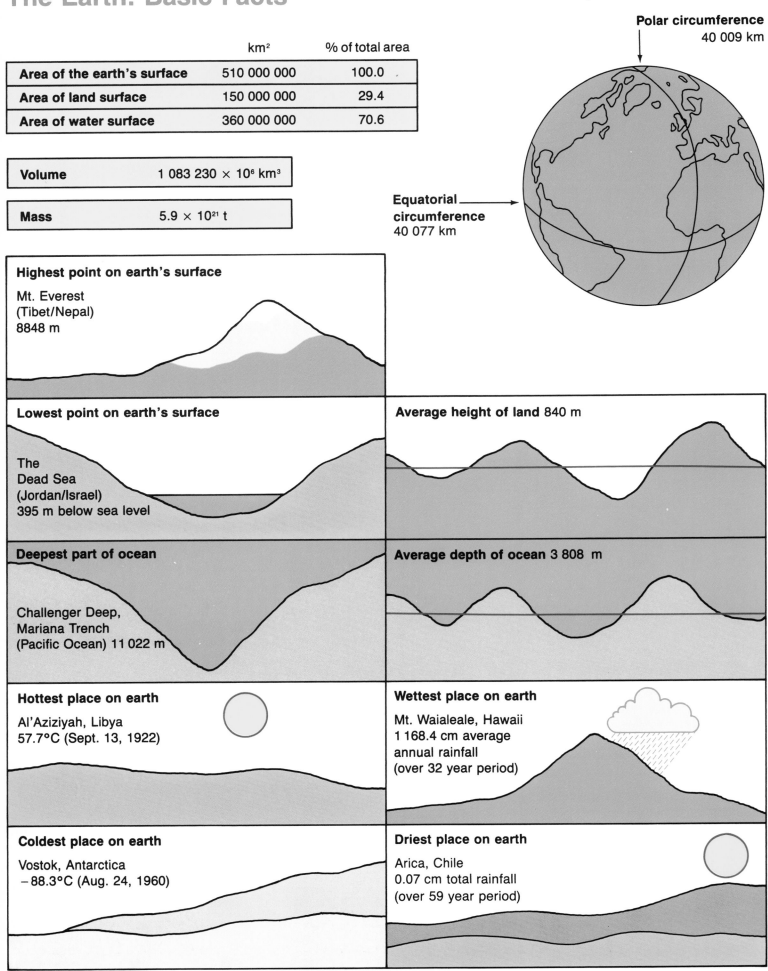

Polar circumference
40 009 km

Equatorial circumference
40 077 km

Highest point on earth's surface

Mt. Everest
(Tibet/Nepal)
8848 m

Lowest point on earth's surface

The
Dead Sea
(Jordan/Israel)
395 m below sea level

Average height of land 840 m

Deepest part of ocean

Challenger Deep,
Mariana Trench
(Pacific Ocean) 11 022 m

Average depth of ocean 3 808 m

Hottest place on earth

Al'Aziziyah, Libya
57.7°C (Sept. 13, 1922)

Wettest place on earth

Mt. Waialeale, Hawaii
1 168.4 cm average
annual rainfall
(over 32 year period)

Coldest place on earth

Vostok, Antarctica
−88.3°C (Aug. 24, 1960)

Driest place on earth

Arica, Chile
0.07 cm total rainfall
(over 59 year period)

The Continents

Continent	Area (km²)	Population	Population/ km²	Country with largest population	Population	Population/ km²
North America	24 241 000	427 226 000	13.0	United States	249 224 000	27.0
South America	17 793 000	296 716 000	17.0	Brazil	150 368 000	18.0
Europe	9 957 000	498 371 000	96.0	Russia*	288 600 000	13.0
Asia	44 500 000	3 112 695 000	113.0	China	1 139 060 000	119.0
Australasia	8 557 000	26 481 000	3.0	Australia	16 873 000	2.0
Africa	30 302 000	642 111 000	21.0	Nigeria	108 542 000	117.0
Antarctica	14 245 000	No permanent population				

*Figures for the population of the European part of Russia (see map on page 1) are not, at present, available. The figure given here is therefore for Russia as a whole.

Principal Mountains of the World

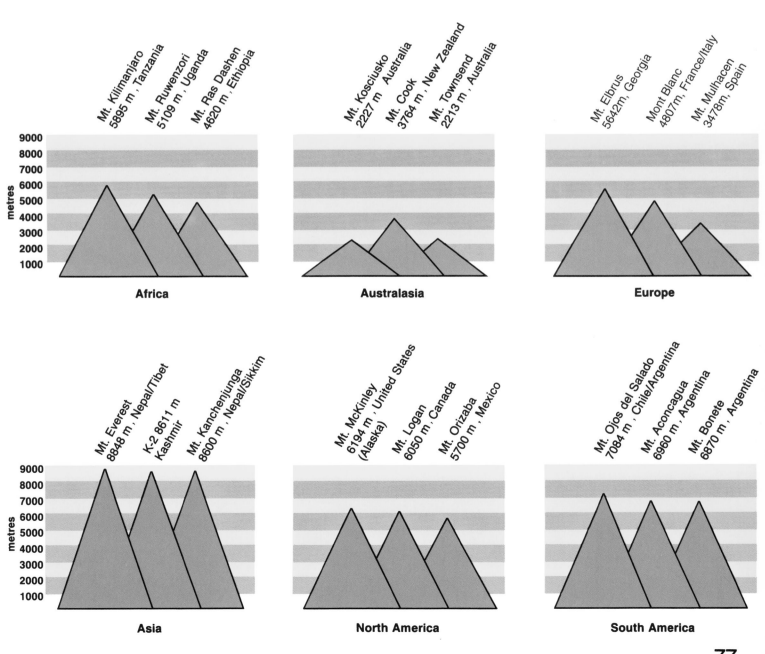

Longest Rivers of the World

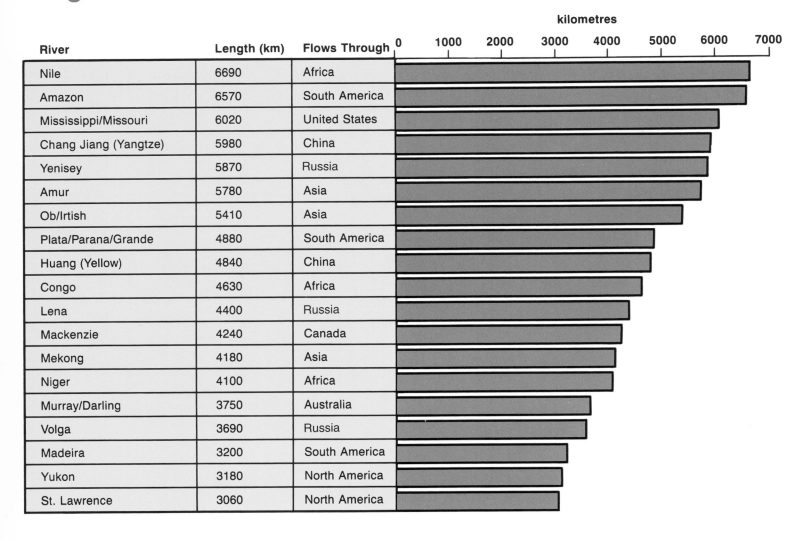

River	Length (km)	Flows Through
Nile	6690	Africa
Amazon	6570	South America
Mississippi/Missouri	6020	United States
Chang Jiang (Yangtze)	5980	China
Yenisey	5870	Russia
Amur	5780	Asia
Ob/Irtish	5410	Asia
Plata/Parana/Grande	4880	South America
Huang (Yellow)	4840	China
Congo	4630	Africa
Lena	4400	Russia
Mackenzie	4240	Canada
Mekong	4180	Asia
Niger	4100	Africa
Murray/Darling	3750	Australia
Volga	3690	Russia
Madeira	3200	South America
Yukon	3180	North America
St. Lawrence	3060	North America

Major Lakes and Inland Seas

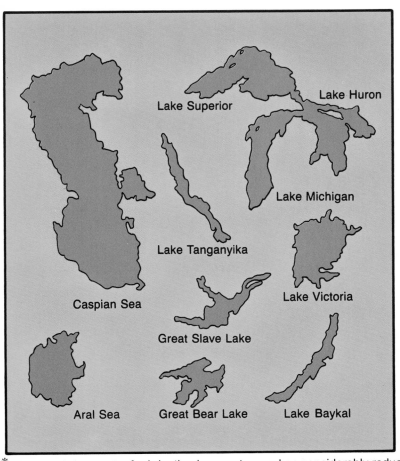

Lake or Sea	Location	Area (km²)
Caspian (salt)	Asia	371 000
Superior	North America	82 260
Aral (salt)	Asia	64 500*
Victoria	Africa	62 940
Huron	North America	59 580
Michigan	United States	58 020
Tanganyika	Africa	32 000
Baykal	Russia	31 500
Great Bear	Canada	31 330
Great Slave	Canada	28 570
Erie	North America	25 710
Winnipeg	Canada	24 390
Malawi	Africa	22 490
Balkhash (salt)	Kazakhstan	17 000–22 000
Ontario	North America	19 270
Ladoga	Russia	18 130
Chad	Africa	10 360–25 900
Maracaibo	Venezuela	13 010
Onega	Russia	9 700
Eyre (salt)	Australia	9 600

*The use of river water for irrigation in recent years has considerably reduced the size of this inland sea from the figures shown in the table.

Oceans and Major Seas

Ocean or Sea	Area (km²)	Mean Depth (m)	Greatest Depth (m)
Pacific	165 760 000	3800	11 500
Atlantic	82 360 000	3500	9200
Indian	73 560 000	4200	8260
Arctic	13 990 000	1200	4880
South China	3 685 000	1650	5514
Caribbean	1 943 000	2230	7492
Mediterranean	2 505 000	1450	4846
Bering	1 943 000	1430	7492

WORLD SOCIAL AND ECONOMIC PATTERNS

World Population: 1650-2000

- ■ Asia
- □ Africa
- ■ Europe (Including U.S.S.R.)
- ■ North America
- ■ South America
- ■ Australasia

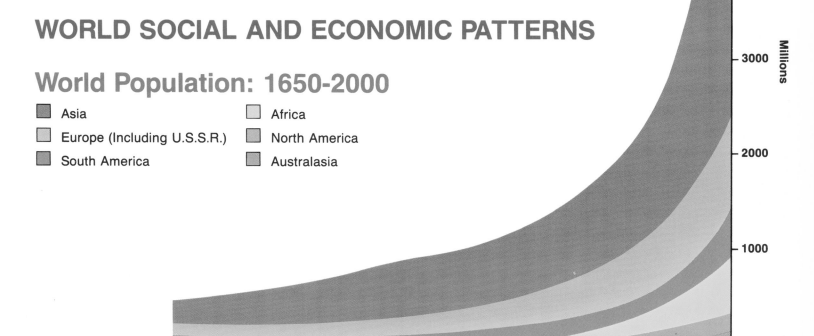

Urban/Rural Population: Selected Countries

Country	Population	Percentage
United Kingdom	57 237 000	93.0%
India	827 057 000	28.0%
Bangladesh	115 593 000	14.0%
Brazil	150 368 000	77.0%
Australia	16 873 000	86.0%
China	1 139 060 000	21.0%
Canada	26 521 000	76.0%
United States	249 224 000	74.0%
Spain	39 187 000	78.0%
Japan	123 460 000	77.0%
Peru	22 330 000	70.0%
Nigeria	108 542 000	35.0%
Kenya	24 031 000	24.0%
Argentina	32 322 000	86.0%
Zaïre	35 568 000	40.0%

■ Percentage of population that lives in towns or cities   ■ Percentage of population that lives in the countryside

Major Cities of the World

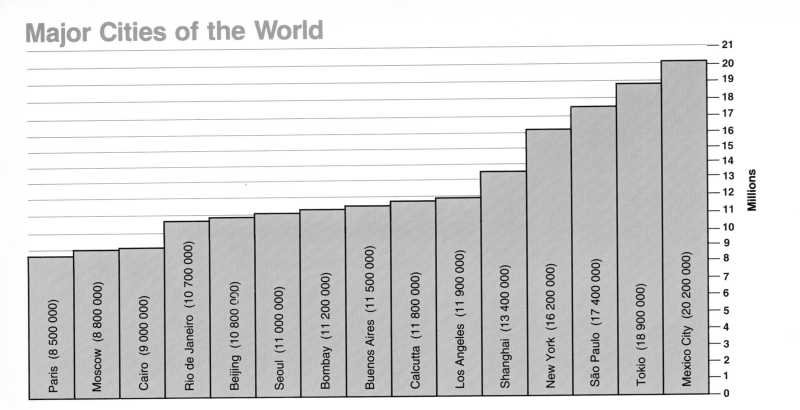

Paris (8 500 000), Moscow (8 800 000), Cairo (9 000 000), Rio de Janeiro (10 700 000), Beijing (10 800 000), Seoul (11 000 000), Bombay (11 200 000), Buenos Aires (11 500 000), Calcutta (11 800 000), Los Angeles (11 900 000), Shanghai (13 400 000), New York (16 200 000), São Paulo (17 400 000), Tokio (18 900 000), Mexico City (20 200 000)

Millions

HEALTH, NUTRITION AND EDUCATION: SELECTED COUNTRIES

Literacy*

☐ % Literate   ☐ % Illiterate

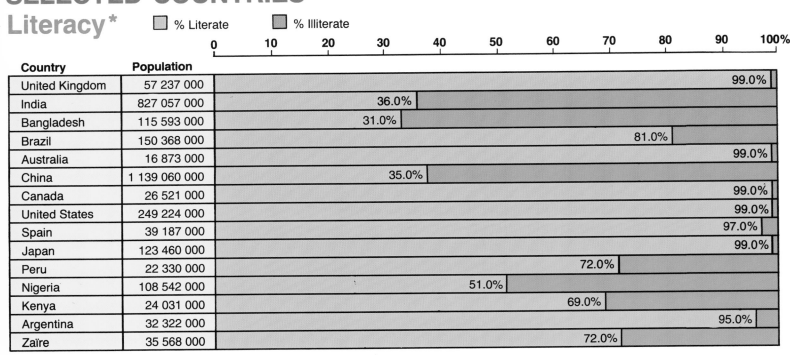

Country	Population	% Literate
United Kingdom	57 237 000	99.0%
India	827 057 000	36.0%
Bangladesh	115 593 000	31.0%
Brazil	150 368 000	81.0%
Australia	16 873 000	99.0%
China	1 139 060 000	35.0%
Canada	26 521 000	99.0%
United States	249 224 000	99.0%
Spain	39 187 000	97.0%
Japan	123 460 000	99.0%
Peru	22 330 000	72.0%
Nigeria	108 542 000	51.0%
Kenya	24 031 000	69.0%
Argentina	32 322 000	95.0%
Zaïre	35 568 000	72.0%

*The percentage of population (over fifteen years of age) able to read

Life Expectancy*

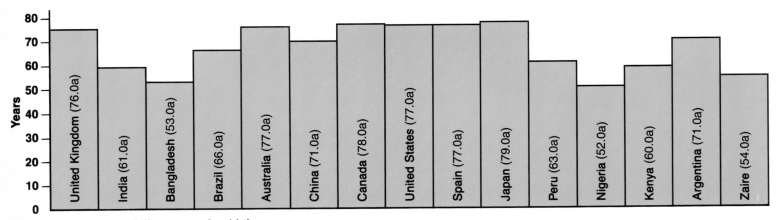

Years

United Kingdom (76.0a), India (61.0a), Bangladesh (53.0a), Brazil (66.0a), Australia (77.0a), China (71.0a), Canada (78.0a), United States (77.0a), Spain (77.0a), Japan (79.0a), Peru (63.0a), Nigeria (52.0a), Kenya (60.0a), Argentina (71.0a), Zaire (54.0a)

*The average length of life expected at birth

Diet and Nutrition

Source: ☐ % Vegetable   ☐ % Animal

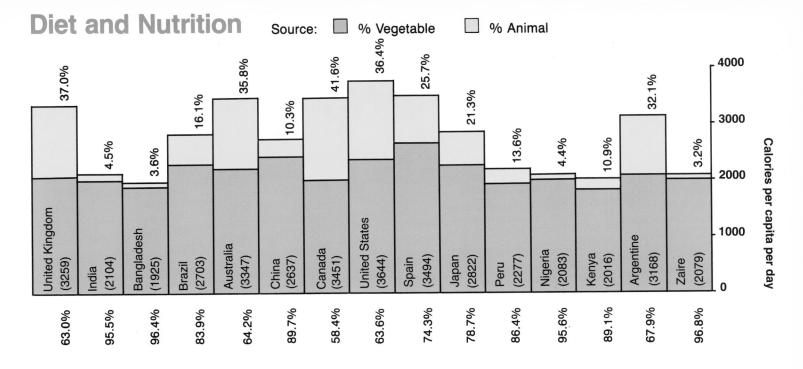

Country	% Animal (top)	% Vegetable (bottom)
United Kingdom (3259)	37.0%	63.0%
India (2104)	4.5%	95.5%
Bangladesh (1925)	3.6%	96.4%
Brazil (2703)	16.1%	83.9%
Australia (3347)	35.8%	64.2%
China (2637)	10.3%	89.7%
Canada (3451)	41.6%	58.4%
United States (3644)	36.4%	63.6%
Spain (3494)	25.7%	74.3%
Japan (2822)	21.3%	78.7%
Peru (2277)	13.6%	86.4%
Nigeria (2083)	4.4%	95.6%
Kenya (2016)	10.9%	89.1%
Argentine (3168)	32.1%	67.9%
Zaire (2079)	3.2%	96.8%

Calories per capita per day

WORLD ENERGY RESOURCES

In the absence of statistics for each of the independent republics of the Commonwealth of Independent States, the figures given here and in the following pages are for the former U.S.S.R. as a whole.

World Energy Reserves

A North America
B Western Europe
C Japan, N.Z., Australia
D U.S.S.R., China
E Latin America
F Middle East and North Africa
G Central and Southern Africa
H South and Eastern Asia

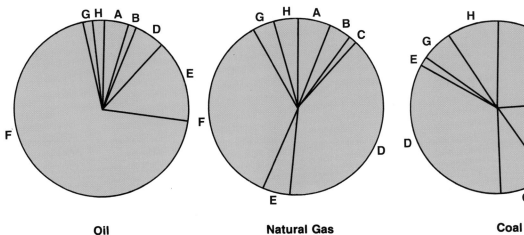

Oil   Natural Gas   Coal

Major Energy Producers

kWh = kilowatt hours   t = tonnes   m³ = cubic metres

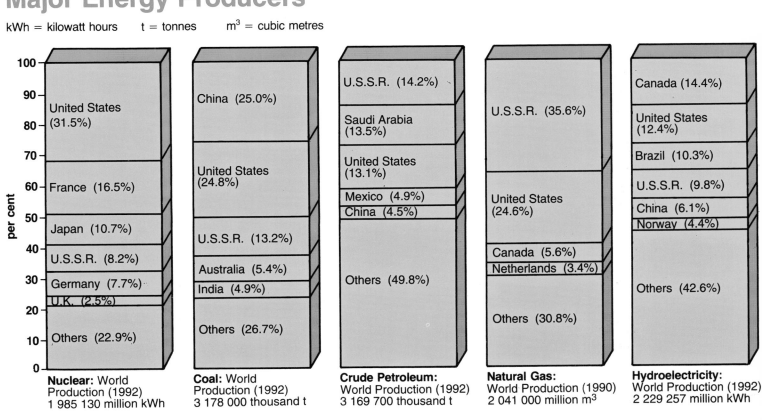

Nuclear: World Production (1992) 1 985 130 million kWh
- United States (31.5%)
- France (16.5%)
- Japan (10.7%)
- U.S.S.R. (8.2%)
- Germany (7.7%)
- U.K. (2.5%)
- Others (22.9%)

Coal: World Production (1992) 3 178 000 thousand t
- China (25.0%)
- United States (24.8%)
- U.S.S.R. (13.2%)
- Australia (5.4%)
- India (4.9%)
- Others (26.7%)

Crude Petroleum: World Production (1992) 3 169 700 thousand t
- U.S.S.R. (14.2%)
- Saudi Arabia (13.5%)
- United States (13.1%)
- Mexico (4.9%)
- China (4.5%)
- Others (49.8%)

Natural Gas: World Production (1990) 2 041 000 million m³
- U.S.S.R. (35.6%)
- United States (24.6%)
- Canada (5.6%)
- Netherlands (3.4%)
- Others (30.8%)

Hydroelectricity: World Production (1992) 2 229 257 million kWh
- Canada (14.4%)
- United States (12.4%)
- Brazil (10.3%)
- U.S.S.R. (9.8%)
- China (6.1%)
- Norway (4.4%)
- Others (42.6%)

WORLD ECONOMIC PATTERNS

World Mineral Production

t = tonnes

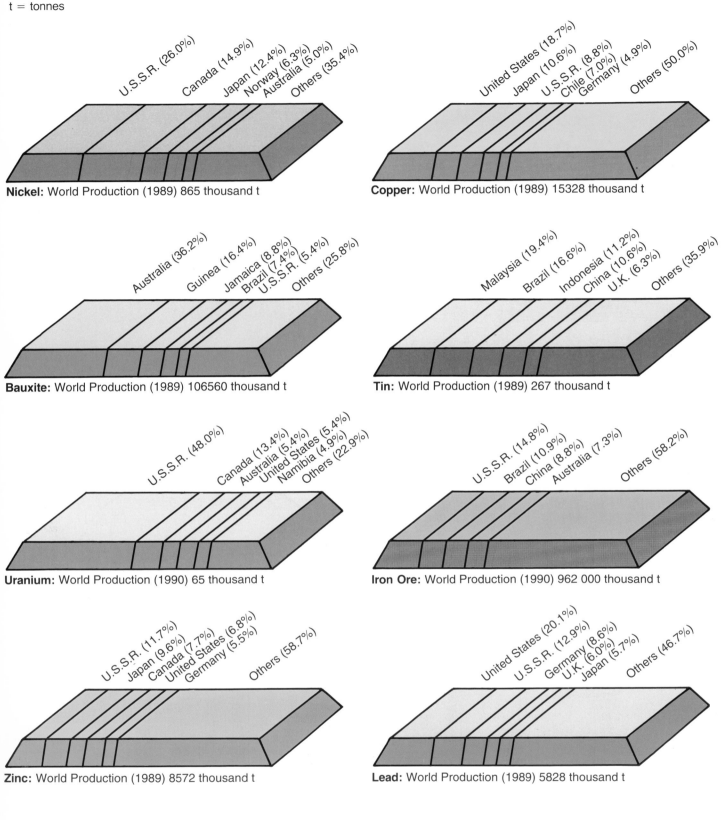

Nickel: World Production (1989) 865 thousand t
- U.S.S.R. (26.0%)
- Canada (14.9%)
- Japan (12.4%)
- Norway (6.3%)
- Australia (5.0%)
- Others (35.4%)

Copper: World Production (1989) 15328 thousand t
- United States (18.7%)
- Japan (10.6%)
- U.S.S.R. (8.8%)
- Chile (7.0%)
- Germany (4.9%)
- Others (50.0%)

Bauxite: World Production (1989) 106560 thousand t
- Australia (36.2%)
- Guinea (16.4%)
- Jamaica (8.8%)
- Brazil (7.4%)
- U.S.S.R. (5.4%)
- Others (25.8%)

Tin: World Production (1989) 267 thousand t
- Malaysia (19.4%)
- Brazil (16.6%)
- Indonesia (11.2%)
- China (10.6%)
- U.K. (6.3%)
- Others (35.9%)

Uranium: World Production (1990) 65 thousand t
- U.S.S.R. (48.0%)
- Canada (13.4%)
- Australia (5.4%)
- United States (5.4%)
- Namibia (4.9%)
- Others (22.9%)

Iron Ore: World Production (1990) 962 000 thousand t
- U.S.S.R. (14.8%)
- Brazil (10.9%)
- China (8.8%)
- Australia (7.3%)
- Others (58.2%)

Zinc: World Production (1989) 8572 thousand t
- U.S.S.R. (11.7%)
- Japan (9.6%)
- Canada (7.7%)
- United States (6.8%)
- Germany (5.5%)
- Others (58.7%)

Lead: World Production (1989) 5828 thousand t
- United States (20.1%)
- U.S.S.R. (12.9%)
- Germany (8.6%)
- U.K. (6.0%)
- Japan (5.7%)
- Others (46.7%)

Steel

World Production (1989)
685 000 thousand t

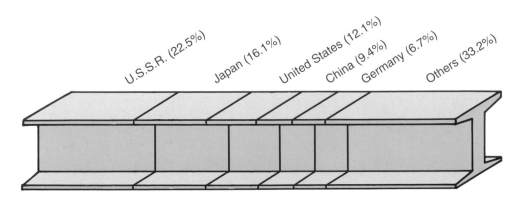

- U.S.S.R. (22.5%)
- Japan (16.1%)
- United States (12.1%)
- China (9.4%)
- Germany (6.7%)
- Others (33.2%)

82

AGRICULTURE

Arable Land: Selected Countries

☐ % Arable* ■ % Non-arable

Country	Total Land Area (km²)	% Arable
United Kingdom	242 000	28.7%
India	2 973 000	55.8%
Bangladesh	130 000	69.1%
Brazil	8 457 000	←7.9%
Australia	7 618 000	←6.1%
China	9 326 000	10.0%
Canada	9 161 000	←5.0%
United States	9 167 000	20.5%
Spain	499 000	31.2%
Japan	377 000	11.1%
Peru	1 280 000	←2.7%
Nigeria	911 000	31.6%
Kenya	570 000	←3.4%
Argentina	2 737 000	9.5%
Zaïre	2 267 000	←3.2%

*Arable land is land suitable for cultivation of crops. It does not include pasture and woodland.

World Food Production

t=tonnes

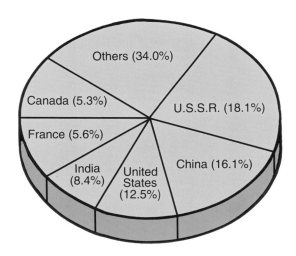

Wheat: World Production (1990) 595 652 thousand t

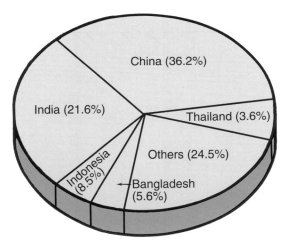

Rice: World Production (1990) 520 513 thousand t

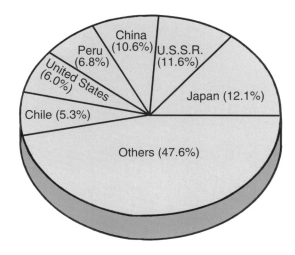

Fish: World Catch (1988) 97 985 thousand t

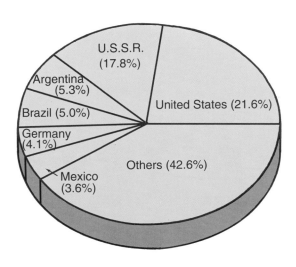

Beef: World Production (1989) 49 436 thousand t

INDEX

This index contains the names of places shown on the regional maps in the Atlas. Names that appear on more than one map are indexed only once, to the most appropriate scale.

The page number is given first in bold type. The reference numbers that follow also appear on the left- and right-hand edges of each map, and the letters are at the top and bottom. Where a feature extends over more than one area or crosses a political boundary, the area in which it is most easily located is given.

ABBREVIATIONS:

r. river
l. lake
pen. peninsula
mt. mountain
U.K. United Kingdom
U.S.A. United States of America

85

90